TOOLS

FOR
A SUCCESSFUL
SCHOOL YEAR
(STARTING ON DAY ONE)

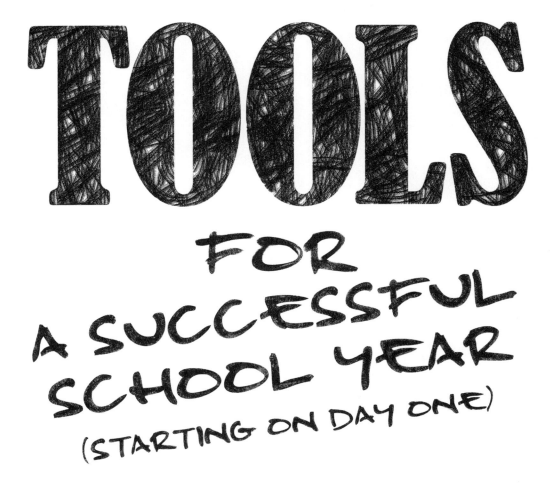

TOOLS
FOR A SUCCESSFUL SCHOOL YEAR
(STARTING ON DAY ONE)

Classroom-Ready Techniques for Building the Four Cornerstones of an Effective Classroom

Over 20 tools for

- Establishing organization, rules, and procedures
- Building positive relationships
- Increasing engagement and enjoyment
- Developing a culture of thinking and learning

Harvey F. Silver | Matthew J. Perini | Abigail L. Boutz

Silver Strong & Associates
Thoughtful Education Press

Silver Strong & Associates
Thoughtful Education Press

3 Tice Road, Suite 2
Franklin Lakes, NJ 07417
Phone: 800-962-4432 or 201-652-1155
Fax: 201-652-1127
Website: www.ThoughtfulClassroom.com
Email: questions@thoughtfulclassroom.com

President and Tools Series Developer: Harvey F. Silver
Director of Publishing and Tools Series Editor: Matthew J. Perini
Design and Production Directors: Bethann Carbone & Michael Heil
Proofreaders: Christine Hood & Rachel Rosolina

Some of the reproducibles in this book have been published previously, in other books from the Tools for Today's Educators series. The reproducibles on pages 13, 32, 33, 42, 43, 67, and 69 are reprinted or adapted with permission from *Tools for Thoughtful Assessment* by A. L. Boutz, H. F. Silver, J. W. Jackson, and M. J. Perini, 2012, Franklin Lakes, NJ: Thoughtful Education Press. © 2012 by Silver Strong & Associates. The reproducible on page 79 is reprinted with permission from *Tools for Conquering the Common Core* by H. F. Silver and A. L. Boutz, 2015, Franklin Lakes, NJ: Thoughtful Education Press. © 2015 by Silver Strong & Associates.

All web links in this book are correct as of the publication date below but may have become inactive or otherwise modified since that time. If you notice a deactivated or changed link, please email questions@thoughtfulclassroom.com with the words "Link Update" in the subject line. In your message, please specify the web link, the book title, and the page number on which the link appears.

Printed in the United States of America

Quantity discounts are available. For information, call 800-962-4432.

ISBN: 978-1-58284-209-7
Library of Congress Control Number: 2016935338

23 22 21 20 19 18 17 16   4 5 6 7 8 9 10

Acknowledgments

As always, we are extremely grateful to the teachers, students, and administrators who have piloted our tools in their schools and provided us with valuable feedback. We would particularly like to acknowledge Children's Aid College Prep Charter School (Bronx, NY); Lyman Hall Elementary School (Gainesville, GA); Red Mesa Unified School District #27 (Arizona); University Prep Charter High School (Bronx, NY); Williamsville Central School District (New York); and the educators and administrators from the West Babylon School District (New York) who were involved in contributing to and supporting the discussion of tools from the Tools for Today's Educators series on their Reflective Pathway blog, especially the blog's moderator, Lisa Granieri.

Special thanks go out to our colleague, Beth Knoedelseder, whose work inspired and enhanced several tools in this book. We would also like to acknowledge the thoughtful feedback provided by Edward Thomas and to thank Justin Gilbert, Trisha Layden, Kimberly Nunez, and Irena Rothaug for their help and support with various production, publishing, and permissions-related tasks.

For copies of the reproducibles
and other downloadable extras noted in the text,
visit **www.ThoughtfulClassroom.com/Tools**.

Contents

Welcome to "Tools for Today's Educators"

The book you're holding in your hands is part of Tools for Today's Educators, a series that we began publishing more than a decade ago. We began creating tools—classroom-ready techniques for improving teaching and learning—because the teachers we worked with were asking us for simple but effective solutions for problems they faced in their classrooms. They wanted practical techniques for addressing these problems, not theoretical ones; techniques that they could implement quickly, without a lot of advance planning; and techniques that could be adapted for use in different grade levels and content areas. Most of all, they wanted techniques that would work in real classrooms with real students.

Over the years, we've kept these requests in mind as we developed the various books in our Tools line. We've also continued to ask teachers about the challenges they face in their classrooms, so that we can provide them with tools for addressing those challenges. This particular book was inspired by requests for tools that could be used to lay the foundation for a successful school year and then build on that foundation all year long. Like all our Tools books, it was designed to promote better teaching, better learning, and student engagement.

Let us know how the tools are working for you and your students. We'd love to hear from you!

Harvey F. Silver
Series Developer

Matthew J. Perini
Series Editor

Introduction: Make This Year *That* Year

Think back for a moment on *that* school year, your very favorite year as a teacher—that year when you came home each night exhilarated, just raring to get back into the classroom the next day. Or, if you're a new teacher, imagine what that ideal school year will be like. Whether you're drawing on experience or imagination, we're betting you're envisioning something like this: The classroom isn't just orderly; it operates as a learning community. Students aren't just on task; they're highly engaged in their learning. Student achievement isn't just "meeting benchmarks"; it consistently reflects deep understanding and high-quality thinking. This book is about how to make every year *that* year, starting on the very first day of school.

What Makes This Book Different?

Clearly, this is not the first book on how to begin the school year so that the conditions for yearlong success are in place early on. But it is a unique one. Three features in particular set this book apart from other resources dedicated to helping teachers get off on the right foot.

The first distinguishing feature of this book is its scope. Many books about the beginning of the school year place a relatively narrow emphasis on classroom management. This book encourages teachers to take a broader, bolder, and more dynamic approach—one that's designed to ensure order, yes, but also to make learning exciting, create a strong learning community, and help students become better thinkers.

Why do we advocate this broader approach? Because research on teacher effectiveness shows that a successful classroom is much more than a well-managed classroom. By conducting a deep analysis of preeminent teacher effectiveness frameworks and standards (Council of Chief State School Officers, 2011; Danielson, 2013; Marzano, 2013; Stronge, 2010) and working with hundreds of teachers to convert the research into a simple and practical classroom model, we have found that all successful classrooms rest on what we call the Four Cornerstones of Effective Classrooms.* These are the Four Cornerstones:

1. Organization, Rules, and Procedures

2. Positive Relationships

3. Engagement and Enjoyment

4. A Culture of Thinking and Learning

These Four Cornerstones are the non-negotiables of a truly successful learning environment—those universal elements that we find in all highly effective classrooms. Thus, laying down these cornerstones early is the key to a successful school year.

---

*The Four Cornerstones are a key component of the Thoughtful Classroom Teacher Effectiveness Framework (Silver Strong & Associates, 2012). For more information about this framework, see the Appendix.

For each cornerstone, we have devised an essential question that clarifies the goal of the cornerstone and that can help focus your thinking about how to create the best learning environment possible. Here are the essential questions associated with the Four Cornerstones:

1. **Organization, Rules, and Procedures:** How can I organize my classroom to enhance learning and establish rules and procedures that clarify expectations?

2. **Positive Relationships:** How can I build meaningful relationships with students and among students to promote learning?

3. **Engagement and Enjoyment:** How can I motivate students to do their best work and inspire the love of learning?

4. **A Culture of Thinking and Learning:** How can I develop a classroom culture that promotes serious learning and sophisticated forms of thinking?

We encourage you to use these essential questions as your guides to a successful school year. Begin by thinking about your current practice: What are you already doing to support each cornerstone in your classroom? Which cornerstones might need more attention? Then, decide how you will respond. As much as possible, conduct this process of analyzing your current practice and exploring potential responses with your colleagues, so that you can learn from one another and develop plans for improving together.

Of course, when it comes to the challenge of responding—of translating strategic reflection into meaningful classroom practice—essential questions are not enough. This recognition brings us to the second distinguishing feature of the book, a feature that can be summed up in a single word: *how*. Many books on improving classroom practice tell teachers what to do, but far fewer show them how. This book provides the *how* in the form of classroom-ready tools for targeting each cornerstone.

In Chapter 1, you'll find tools to help you establish organization, rules, and procedures that promote positive behavior and high levels of learning. The tools in Chapter 2 will help you foster meaningful relationships in your classroom, including the relationships you build with your students and the kinds of student-student relationships that characterize a strong learning community. Use the tools in Chapter 3, which focuses on engagement and enjoyment, to make your classroom a more dynamic, motivating, and exciting place for students to learn. And turn to Chapter 4 for tools that can help you develop a classroom culture that is characterized by sophisticated thinking and deep learning.

The third distinguishing feature of this book can be gleaned from its title: *Tools for a Successful School Year (Starting on Day One)*. While the tools in this book are designed to help you start the year off right, nearly all of them are every bit as useful in January or April as they are in September. So, while it's important to get the Four Cornerstones in place as early as possible, you shouldn't feel pressured to put every tool into practice during the first month of school. Instead, think of this book as a full-year resource for promoting classroom success—but one that gets a few more dog-eared pages early on.

Key Design Features of This Book

To help you understand what the book contains and how to use it effectively, we've summarized some of its key design features in the sections that follow.

Designed to work for busy teachers

We know how busy teachers are, and we structured this book accordingly. Specifically:

We kept things short and simple so that tools could be put into practice quickly. A description of each tool, its benefits, and steps for implementing it can all be found on a single page. Most tools require little or no advance planning, and all have seven steps or fewer.

We formatted each tool so that critical information would be easy to find and use. Every tool contains the same four basic sections (see box below). Large, boldface headings let you jump to whichever sections you're interested in, and in whatever order works best for you.

Every tool contains the same four basic sections:

1. **What is it?**
   A brief description of the tool and its purpose

2. **What are the benefits?**
   A one-paragraph explanation of how the tool enhances teaching, learning, and/or student behavior

3. **What are the basic steps?**
   A step-by-step description of how to implement the tool in the classroom; for ease of use, each tool includes seven steps or fewer

4. **How is the tool used in the classroom?**
   A section that provides greater clarity on how the tool can be used and typically includes specific examples from different grade levels and content areas

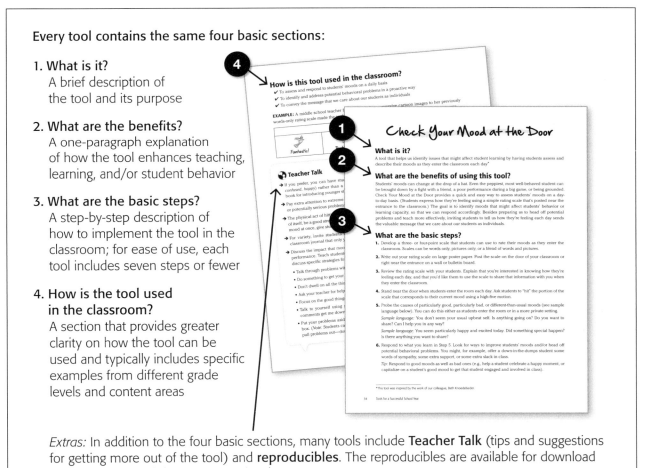

Extras: In addition to the four basic sections, many tools include **Teacher Talk** (tips and suggestions for getting more out of the tool) and **reproducibles**. The reproducibles are available for download at www.ThoughtfulClassroom.com/Tools.

We provided everything you need to get the tools going in your classroom. Besides the essentials, like easy-to-follow steps and ready-to-go reproducibles (available both in the book and on the book's companion website, www.ThoughtfulClassroom.com/Tools), many tools include Teacher Talk—a bonus section filled with teacher tips, implementation suggestions, and other useful information. Skimming the Teacher Talk section before trying a tool for the first time can help you avoid potential pitfalls and start using the tool like an expert.

We designed the book to be easily searchable, so you don't have to read it from cover to cover. Skim the one-sentence "What is it?" descriptions to find a tool that meets your needs, or use one of the book's search features:

- Use the Table of Contents (p. vii) to find tools for addressing each individual cornerstone. Keep in mind, though, that many tools can help you address more than one cornerstone.

- Use the chapter introductions (pp. 9–10, 27–28, 51–52, and 81–82) to get a quick, thumbnail description of each tool, so you can decide which tools are right for you and your students.

- Use the Index of Tools (p. 117) to search for tools by name.

Designed to work in real classrooms

The tools in this book are aligned with important research on teacher effectiveness. More than that, though, they're designed to work in real classrooms with real students. To get the tools working in *your* classroom, be sure to review them thoroughly (including classroom examples and teacher tips), modify them as needed, and use them regularly. Stop after each use to reflect on how things went and steps you might take to make the tool work even better the next time you use it.

To facilitate this kind of reflection, we've included a simple reflection form and guidelines for creating a reflection journal in the Epilogue (pp. 109–110). Whenever possible, engage in the reflective process with your colleagues, so that you can learn from each other's experiences and offer each other suggestions. ("The way I simplified this tool to make it work for my struggling readers was ...")

Designed to be used across grade levels and content areas

Every classroom should be a Four Cornerstones classroom. Whether you are teaching kindergarten or AP Biology, your classroom will benefit from clear organization, strong relationships, engaged students, and a focus on thinking and learning. That's why we've included tools that can be used across content areas and grade levels—and classroom examples that reflect this diversity. Use the examples to see how tools can be adapted to meet specific content and classroom demands.

Designed to be used with colleagues

Creating and sustaining a Four Cornerstones classroom can be challenging. The good news is that you don't have to do it alone. Because this book can be used across grade levels and content areas, you and your colleagues can support each other as you learn, practice, and refine your use of individual tools. Build staff meetings and conversations around particular cornerstones and particular tools that address those cornerstones. Commit to trying a new tool on a regular basis with your professional learning community (PLC). Or, do what a group of educators in West Babylon, New York, did and create a blog where teachers can share and learn from each other's experiences with specific tools (http://reflectivepathway.blogspot.com).

Committing to learning tools with your colleagues will help you implement the tools more confidently and address the Four Cornerstones more effectively. Think, for example, how much better students will be at following key rules and procedures or developing important thinking skills if everyone in your school has been working to develop these capacities. And consider how much richer the conversations will be among staff members if every teacher is using a common set of tools to develop these behaviors and skills from the earliest grades on up.

Designed to be used by administrators as well as teachers

The tools in this book aren't just designed to help teachers; they're designed to help administrators grow their capacities as instructional leaders. Principals and other school leaders can use the tools to provide teachers with concrete suggestions for targeting individual cornerstones and improving their classroom practice. This process is beneficial when used with individual teachers ("When I observed your lesson, I noticed that a few students seemed confused about how to complete the task. A tool like 7-Step Directions might help ensure that all students are clear about what to do before they get started") or as part of a schoolwide initiative to target particular cornerstones ("It seems like a lot of teachers are really working hard to increase engagement in their classrooms. Over the next month, let's all commit to using at least two tools from the Engagement and Enjoyment chapter"). Note that deciding to address a particular tool or cornerstone schoolwide is a great way to get everyone on the same page and ensure that classroom goals are aligned with school goals.

Designed to support the goals of PBIS

Many educators across the country are working to implement positive behavioral interventions and supports (PBIS) in their classrooms, schools, and districts. At the heart of the PBIS framework is the well-established idea that a positive and preventive approach to behavior management leads to far better outcomes than reactive or punishment-based approaches. This book directly supports, at the classroom level, the kind of proactive approach to behavior management that PBIS calls for.

The table below highlights several evidence-based classroom practices that have been found to have a positive impact on student behavior (Simonsen, Fairbanks, Briesch, Myers, & Sugai, 2008; US Office of Special Education Programs, 2015). It also identifies key tools from this book that can help you put these practices to work in your classroom.

Practices that promote positive behavior	Key tools that support each practice
Teaching classroom routines and procedures directly	• Procedural PRO (pp. 14–17) • Say "S" to Resolving Conflicts (pp. 48–50)
Posting classroom expectations and teaching them explicitly; involving students in defining those expectations	• Respectfully Yours (pp. 18–19) • Rules to Live and Learn By (pp. 20–22)
Outlining the steps for completing specific activities	• 7-Step Directions (pp. 11–13)
Using praise to recognize and reinforce positive student behaviors	• Respectfully Yours (pp. 18–19) • Rules to Live and Learn By (pp. 20–22)
Providing multiple and varied opportunities for students to respond	• Community CIRCLE (pp. 36–38) • Interaction in an Instant (pp. 44–47) • Questioning in Style (pp. 70–75)
Posting materials that support critical content and learning strategies	• Student-Friendly Learning Targets (pp. 23–25) • 3C Word Walls (pp. 83–89) • Power Previewing (pp. 103–107)

Note that the list of tools on the previous page isn't exhaustive. It only includes tools that employ the specific practices featured in the table, not tools that support the broader PBIS goal of managing student behavior proactively (see, for example, the Check Your Mood at the Door tool from Chapter 2). Indeed, since PBIS experts Brandi Simonsen and Diane Myers (2015) remind us that "good instruction is one of [a teacher's] best behavior management tools" (p. 16), we would argue that all the tools in this book—not just the ones that are directly aligned to specific PBIS practices—can help you on your quest to improve student behavior.

. . .

Early in this introduction, we invited you to envision the ideal school year. A vision of success is important and can help guide our aspirations as educators. But making that vision a reality requires a *how*—an approach that's practical, that's manageable, and that leads to positive change. We encourage you to see this book as that how. Starting on day one, select and implement the tools you need to make the Four Cornerstones the governing principles of your classroom. We are confident that the results will be noticeable early and will pay off all year long.

1

Establishing Organization, Rules, and Procedures

How can I organize my classroom to enhance learning and establish rules and procedures that clarify expectations?

Organizing is what you do before you do something, so that when you do it, it is not all mixed up.

—A. A. Milne

More than 80 percent of behavior problems in the classroom have nothing to do with discipline. They are related to classrooms that lack procedures and routines.

—Harry K. Wong and Rosemary T. Wong, *The Classroom Management Book*

When we think of well-run classrooms, we think of classrooms that operate efficiently—classrooms where students know what is expected of them as learners, where they understand what it means to be productive classroom contributors, and where they behave accordingly. Needless to say, classrooms like these don't happen by accident. They are the result of deliberate effort on the teacher's part. They are the result of careful organization, thoughtful rules, and explicitly taught procedures.

This chapter focuses on the first cornerstone of effective classrooms: Organization, Rules, and Procedures. As the first cornerstone, it is the prerequisite for all the others. Without this cornerstone in place, precious instructional time gets frittered away, as classroom disturbances and behavioral issues become the norm. But once this cornerstone is established, the routines that support high-level learning become firmly set and the benefits last all year long.

In this chapter, we present five tools that support this critical cornerstone:

1. **7-Step Directions** helps students complete assigned tasks more successfully by using a simple and consistent format to clarify task directions and expectations.

2. **Procedural PRO** spells out a three-step process for helping students execute classroom procedures independently: (1) **P**resent and model the procedure, (2) help students **R**ehearse the procedure, and (3) encourage students to independently execute, or **O**wn, the procedure.

3. **Respectfully Yours** teaches students what it means to show respect for each other, the classroom, and the teacher; in doing so, it empowers students to assess and regulate their own behavior.

4. **Rules to Live and Learn By** invites students to participate in developing classroom behavioral guidelines that promote a positive and productive learning environment.

5. **Student-Friendly Learning Targets** enables students to assess, monitor, and direct their own learning by ensuring that classroom learning expectations are expressed using clear and simple language.

7-Step Directions

What is it?

A seven-question framework that helps students complete their assignments more successfully by clarifying instructions, expectations, and what-to-do-when-stuck strategies before they start working

What are the benefits of using this tool?

When students fail to complete their assignments (or complete them properly), we often assume that a lack of effort, ability, or readiness is to blame. In many cases, however, students fail for an entirely different reason—they fail because they're unclear about what they've been asked to do or how to do it. This tool prevents these kinds of failures from happening and increases time-on-task by clarifying instructions up front. It also prepares students to be more self-directed and successful on future assignments by making them aware of the kinds of questions they should ask themselves before beginning *any* assigned task.

What are the basic steps?

1. Ask yourself the following questions before giving students a homework or classwork assignment:

- WHAT is the assigned task?
- WHO should perform the task? Some students? All students? Pairs of students? Teams?
- WHEN should students start the task? And how long do they have to complete it?
- HOW should students go about completing the task? What steps are involved?
- What should students do if they need HELP? What strategies should they try?
- What should students do AFTER they complete the task?
- What CRITERIA will you use to evaluate students' work?

2. Record your answers on a 7-Step Directions template (p. 13), or write the questions and answers on the board.

3. Review your answers with students before they begin working on the assigned task. Use the "see it and say it" technique to make this review more effective:

> *See it:* Let students see the questions and answers. Depending on what you did in Step 2, this will entail distributing copies of your completed template or calling students' attention to the board.
>
> *Say it:* Go through the questions one at a time. Have students say what the assignment entails by asking them to read the answers aloud or explain the answers in their own words. Address any questions that students have before moving on.

4. Prepare students for future success by teaching them to seek out answers to the 7-Step Directions questions before they begin working on *any* assigned task. Explain that having these answers can help them complete their tasks more successfully.

How is this tool used in the classroom?

✔ To provide clear directions for classroom tasks

✔ To help students complete assigned tasks more efficiently and successfully

✔ To keep the flow of classroom activities moving smoothly

EXAMPLE: A sixth-grade mathematics teacher regularly uses the 7-Step Directions framework to introduce her students' homework assignments. The template that she completed for one of these assignments is shown below.

1) WHAT	Work on tonight's homework assignment: problems 1–10 on p. 45 of your text.
2) WHO	Students who have finished their classwork
3) WHEN	Start working as soon as you finish your classwork. Stop working two minutes before the bell rings so that you have time to pack up your things.
4) HOW	Work on your own or with a partner. Before you begin, review what we've learned about equivalence and applying the properties of operations to generate equivalent expressions. Check your class notes as well as your text.
5) HELP	"Ask three before me."
6) AFTER	Reflect on the assignment. Were the problems hard? Easy? Medium? Why do you think so? Record your thoughts and feelings in your Learning Log, and be prepared to share them in class tomorrow.
7) CRITERIA	Problem sets will be evaluated for completeness and accuracy. All work should be shown.

SOURCE: Adapted from *Tools for Thoughtful Assessment* (p. 45), by A. L. Boutz, H. F. Silver, J. W. Jackson, and M. J. Perini, 2012, Franklin Lakes, NJ: Thoughtful Education Press. © 2012 by Silver Strong & Associates. Adapted with permission.

🔘 Teacher Talk

➔ Teachers who use this tool on a regular basis often leave the seven prompts on the board so they can simply fill in the answers when introducing each new assignment.

➔ If students need help completing an assigned task, you may want to refer them to the "ask three before me" rule. This rule, which states that they should ask three people (e.g., classmates, parents, school librarian) for help before asking you, teaches students to become more self-sufficient. It also promotes collaboration and builds interpersonal skills by encouraging students to seek help from others.

➔ Help students work more efficiently by encouraging them to think about the resources and supplies that assigned tasks require and gather those resources and supplies before they start working.

7-Step Directions

1) WHAT	
2) WHO	
3) WHEN	
4) HOW	
5) HELP	
6) AFTER	
7) CRITERIA	

Procedural PRO

What is it?

A tool that uses direct instruction and guided practice to help students become pros at classroom procedures

What are the benefits of using this tool?

Classroom management experts Harry K. Wong and Rosemary T. Wong (2014) remind us that "procedures are the foundation upon which successful teaching takes place" (p. 6). But having procedures that are clear in *our* minds isn't the same as students having procedures clear in *their* minds. And if students' grasp of important procedures is fuzzy, then the overall effectiveness of the classroom will be compromised. This tool presents a simple, three-phase process for teaching classroom procedures. The three phases, the acronym for which is PRO, empower students to become pros at the various classroom procedures they learn. The three phases also highlight the gradual shift in responsibility that should come with teaching a procedure to students: the teacher **P**resents the procedure, the class **R**ehearses the procedure under the teacher's guidance, and over time, students come to **O**wn (internalize and independently execute) the procedure.

What are the basic steps?

1. Identify a classroom procedure or content-related procedure that you want students to master. Break the procedure into a series of manageable steps.

2. Ask students what it means to be a pro at something. Explain that you're going to use a simple, three-step process to help them become pros at the procedure you identified in Step 1.

3. Use the handout on p. 17 to teach students (and yourself) what the PRO process entails. Help students notice how the PRO process gradually shifts the responsibility of executing the procedure from teacher to students.

4. **P**resent the selected procedure to students in a step-by-step manner. Make sure you

- Introduce the procedure and explain why it's important.
- Explain and model the individual steps. Answer any questions that students might have.
- Walk through the procedure as a class, completing one step at a time. Give students feedback about their performance after each step, and help them make any necessary corrections.

5. Give students multiple opportunities to **R**ehearse the procedure. Observe, coach, and give them feedback as they practice. The goal is to encourage increasing independence over time.

Note: You can have students practice as a class, in small groups or pairs, or independently.

6. Encourage students to **O**wn or take responsibility for following the procedure without help.

7. Acknowledge students who follow the procedure successfully. Identify students who still need help, and continue working with them until they, too, are pros.

How is this tool used in the classroom?

✔ To teach and help students internalize important classroom (and content-related) procedures

EXAMPLE 1: Becoming pros at lining up to leave the classroom*

Before teaching her students the proper procedure for lining up to leave the classroom, a primary-grade teacher divides the procedure into three simple steps:

STEP 1: Stand up and push your chair under your desk.

STEP 2: Be as quiet as a feather when walking toward the door. Walk with "feather feet."

STEP 3: Line up as straight as an arrow.

She explains the importance of lining up quietly and then **P**resents the steps to students. To check that students understand what's expected of them, the teacher has them execute the steps one at a time on her command. ("I'll say, 'Stand up and push your chair under your desk,' but you shouldn't actually do those things until I say, 'Ready, set, GO!'") She checks students' performance after each step and helps students make any necessary corrections ("Let's try to walk more quietly").

The teacher and her students **R**ehearse the lining-up procedure regularly over the next few weeks, using the poem below as a guide. They read the poem one couplet at a time (she reads the first line of the couplet aloud; students chant the second line as a class), and students execute the appropriate step at the conclusion of each couplet. After each rehearsal, the teacher assesses and gives students feedback about their performance: Were students as quiet as a feather? Was their line as straight as an arrow?

> Here's how we begin:
> We stand up and push our chairs in.
> Then, quiet as a feather,
> We walk together.
> Arrow-straight,
> Our line looks great!

After a few weeks of practice, it's clear that students **O**wn the procedure, as evidenced by their ability to execute the steps properly without needing the support of the poem.

EXAMPLE 2: Becoming pros at the order of operations

An elementary teacher uses Procedural PRO to help students become "order of operations pros." He begins by explaining the importance of completing mathematical operations in order. Next, he **P**resents the proper order for completing the various operations using the "Please Excuse My Dear Aunt Sally" mnemonic as a guide. He then models the order of operations procedure for students by working through several specific examples.

Once students have the gist of the procedure, the teacher invites them to **R**ehearse as a class using an example he puts on the board. He instructs students to complete the first step at their seats, while he completes it on the board. When students finish, they look up to check and correct their work and ask for help if needed. The teacher then repeats the process for each successive step.

After several successful practice sessions using increasingly complex examples, students gain the confidence and skill they need to work independently. In other words, they **O**wn the order of operations procedure.

---

*This lesson is adapted from the work of our colleague, Beth Knoedelseder.

EXAMPLE 3: Becoming pros at start-of-class procedures

A sixth-grade teaching team knows that first-year middle schoolers have, for the first time in their academic careers, several different sets of classroom procedures that they need to master. Recognizing that trying to remember the "getting started procedures" for each individual class can be overwhelming for many students, the team agrees that all teachers will create checklists for entering their classrooms. One teacher's checklist is shown here:

What should you do when you enter the classroom?
☐ Take out your learning log, your daily planner, and a pen or pencil.
☐ Look at the side board and copy the homework assignment into your planner.
☐ Make sure you understand the homework assignment. If you have questions, ask me!
☐ Turn in your homework, or complete "the dog ate my homework" sheet.
☐ Start working on the daily warm-up activity.

After **P**resenting their start-of-class procedures to students on the first day of school using the checklists as a guide, the teachers encourage students to check their checklists each day and execute the listed procedures (**R**ehearse). Over time, students become familiar enough with the procedures that they no longer need to consult their checklists. (They **O**wn the overall routine.)

🌑 Teacher Talk

➔ It's true that teaching classroom procedures requires an investment of time up front, but since classrooms without clearly understood procedures are classrooms where instructional time gets wasted and behavioral issues become pervasive, we believe it's a good investment.

➔ Learn (and help students learn) where they are on the pathway to owning a procedure by having them periodically rate their comfort level using a four-point rating scale (1 = I'm just getting started; 2 = I can do this with lots of guidance; 3 = I can do this with some guidance; 4 = I can do this on my own!).

➔ One way to help students keep track of classroom procedures and execute those procedures properly is to help them create "procedures binders" that include steps/summaries. Keep things manageable by ensuring that students' binders always contain ten procedures or fewer.

➔ The on-my-command technique (Silver, Hanson, Strong, & Schwartz, 1996) that's used to present and help students execute the lining-up procedure in Example 1 can be used with virtually any classroom procedure. Simply break the procedure into simple steps, develop a command word or phrase (e.g., "Ready, set, GO!"), and instruct students not to execute any steps until you give the command. Having students stop and wait for your command before executing each step prevents them from jumping ahead. It also gives you the opportunity to assess and correct students' performance *as* they move through the procedure rather than at the end.

➔ Explaining why a procedure is important (see Step 4) is beneficial since students are more apt to follow—or work to master—procedures whose purpose and value they understand.

How to Become a PRO at Procedures

<u>I</u> will … **P**resent the procedure.

- I will introduce the procedure and explain why it's important.

- I will explain and model the steps in the procedure.

- I will ask you to role-play or walk through the basic steps.

- I will check that you understand how to execute the basic steps.

- I will answer any questions that you might have.

<u>WE</u> will … **R**ehearse the procedure.

- We will practice the procedure until everyone feels comfortable with it.

- I will observe you as you practice and help you get better along the way.

- You may ask me questions or ask for help at any time.

<u>YOU</u> will … **O**wn the procedure.

- You will be responsible for following or using the procedure yourself.

Respectfully Yours

What is it?

A tool that helps students behave more respectfully toward you, their classmates, and the classroom by teaching them what respectful behavior does (and doesn't!) look like

What are the benefits of using this tool?

We often ask and expect our students to be respectful, but we don't often teach them what being respectful means. Even when students have a general understanding of what respect means, they're not always clear about what respectful behavior looks like in a classroom setting. This tool helps students grasp the concept of respect and establishes clear behavioral expectations for the classroom by spelling out and modeling what respectful behavior entails.

What are the basic steps?

1. Introduce the concept of respect using any means you choose. See Teacher Talk for ideas.

2. Explain that respect will be a guiding principle in your classroom and that you expect students to respect people's feelings, people's property, and classroom learning time. Ask students to think about what these types of respect might look like. Have them explain or act out their ideas.

3. Use the 3 Cs and 3 Ds (below) to solidify students' grasp of how they should and shouldn't behave in your classroom. Define, discuss, and model (or have students act out) each C and D. Post the Cs and Ds in an easily visible location so students can refer to them throughout the year.

   The 3 Cs of Considerate Behavior
   Considering other people's feelings before speaking or acting
   Contributing to classroom discussions and activities in a positive manner
   Caring for classroom materials and other people's property

   The 3 Ds of Disrespectful Behavior
   Disrespecting your classmates or teacher
   Disrupting classroom learning time
   Damaging classroom materials or other people's property

4. Decide on and discuss the consequences for disrespectful behavior. Consequences should be clear, fair, consistent, and logical. See Teacher Talk for more on establishing consequences.

5. Explain that students are expected to take responsibility for their own behavior. Remind them to use the 3 Cs and 3 Ds to guide their decisions and actions. ("Stop and think: Is what you're about to do or say respectful of me, your classmates, your classroom, and our time together?")

6. Acknowledge students' use of the 3 Cs over the course of the year. Be specific when offering praise so that students are clear about what they've done well. ("I appreciate how your critique was so considerate of Jill's feelings.")

7. Prompt students to correct disrespectful behaviors before implementing consequences. ("Can you reframe your critique in a way that's more considerate of Jill's feelings?")

How is this tool used in the classroom?

✔ To develop students' understanding of what respectful behavior entails

✔ To establish clear behavioral expectations for the classroom

🌑 Teacher Talk

➔ The way you choose to introduce the respect concept in Step 1 will depend on your students' existing knowledge level. Here are some options:

- Define and use concrete examples to help students grasp the concept ("Being respectful means…" "When someone respects another person, he or she…" "When someone respects classroom materials, he or she…"). Test students' ability to distinguish respectful versus disrespectful behavior by describing or acting out specific behaviors and having students hold up *yes* or *no* cards. (Yes, that's an example of being respectful, or no, that's not.)

- Use age-appropriate books to illustrate the notion of behaving respectfully and treating other people/things the way you'd want yourself and your things to be treated. A primary-grade teacher, for example, might try Laurie Keller's (2007) *Do Unto Otters: A Book About Manners*.

- Use questions like these to help students explore what they already know about respect:

  — What comes to mind when you think of the word *respect*? What does respect mean?

  — How do you show respect to others? To people's property? To classroom learning time?

  — How does it feel when people don't treat you with respect?

➔ Illustrating the Cs and Ds using sketches like the ones below can help clarify the behaviors for students, particularly younger students, English language learners, and visual learners.

Another way to concretize and help students internalize the 3 Cs is to have them describe specific ways they could achieve each C. For example, "I could **C**ontribute to classroom discussions in a positive way by asking and answering questions, sharing my ideas with the class, and listening and responding to other people's ideas."

➔ Ensure that the consequences you establish for negative behavior in Step 4 are logical, fair, and expressed effectively by confirming that they meet the "3 Rs" (Nelson, 1985). Specifically, check that your consequences are **R**elated to the initial problem behavior, **R**easonable rather than excessive, and communicated in a **R**espectful manner. If a student stuck gum under his desk, for example, a "related" consequence would be to have him clean the gum off, not take a timeout or go to the principal's office. A "reasonable" consequence would involve having the student clean up *his* desk, not clean gum off all the desks in the classroom. And a "respectfully communicated" consequence would be one that is sensitive to the student's feelings and doesn't cause humiliation.

Rules to Live and Learn By

What is it?

A technique for establishing behavioral guidelines that promote a positive learning environment

What are the benefits of using this tool?

Rules to Live and Learn By outlines a simple process whereby teachers and students work together to establish behavioral guidelines for the classroom—guidelines that encourage cooperation, promote respect for others, and most important, facilitate learning. By focusing on rules and guidelines that help students learn rather than get students to behave, the tool transforms classroom rules from a means of instilling discipline to a means of enhancing achievement.

What are the basic steps?

1. Pose the following question at the start of the year: "What is the primary purpose of coming to school?" (The response you want to hear is, "To learn.") Ask students what learning means to them, and record their ideas on the board.

2. Tell students that you'll work hard to help them learn, and that you expect them to do the same. Explain that there are two rules you'd like them to follow, and that the purpose of the rules is to help them learn. Have students meet in small groups to discuss what each rule means to them.

   RULE 1: Be the best student you can be, and learn as much as possible.

   RULE 2: Make the classroom a good place for everyone to live and learn in.

3. Explain that while you created the rules, it's up to students to figure out how to follow the rules. Have students brainstorm a list of things they could do to support each rule (e.g., ask questions in class, listen when others talk, treat classmates with respect), and record their ideas on the board.

4. Fine-tune this list of rule-supporting behaviors (behavioral guidelines) as a class. Help students eliminate or combine similar ideas, express ideas clearly, and replace negative language with positive (guidelines should state what students *should* do rather than what they shouldn't do).

5. Generate and post a final list of behavioral guidelines. Explain and model each guideline.

6. Make classroom rules and guidelines "a way of life" rather than "a first week of school thing."
   - Target specific guidelines for review throughout the year. (Before a problem-solving lesson, you might review guidelines such as *ask questions if you're confused* or *learn from your mistakes*.)
   - Enforce compliance with posted guidelines throughout the year. Invite students to monitor and assess compliance as well. ("How well have *you* been following our guidelines? How has the class as a whole been following our guidelines?") Discuss strategies for improvement if needed.

7. Acknowledge students' efforts to make the classroom a great place in which to live and learn by praising individual students (or the class as a whole) for following agreed-upon guidelines. Be specific so that students are clear about what they've done well.

How is this tool used in the classroom?

✔ To establish rules and guidelines that promote student learning

✔ To involve students in the process of establishing classroom rules and guidelines

EXAMPLE: The ideas that a class of elementary students generated during the initial brainstorming session (Step 3) are shown in the box below.

What can we do to be the best students we can be and learn as much as possible? (Rule 1)

- Participate in class and ask questions.
- Learn from our mistakes.
- Ask for help if we need it.
- Keep trying. Don't give up if we're stuck.
- Check our work to make sure it's complete and done well.

- Practice the things that we learn.
- Make notes in class and study our notes.
- Write down our assignments.
- Find a quiet place to do our homework.
- Listen to and learn from our classmates.

What can we do to make the classroom a good place for everyone to live and learn in? (Rule 2)

- Listen quietly when the teacher or someone else is talking.
- Take good care of books and other classroom supplies.
- Be polite. Say "please," "thank you," and "you're welcome."
- Find something quiet and productive to do when we finish our work.
- Treat other people the way that we want to be treated.

- Don't use "put downs," only "put ups."
- Clean up any messes that we make.
- Help and support our classmates.
- Be friendly to everyone.
- Use people's names when we speak to them.

With their teacher's help, these students refined, cut, and combined the ideas from their original brainstorming session to create the list of official classroom rules and guidelines shown below.

CLASSROOM RULES AND GUIDELINES

RULE 1: Be the best students we can be, and learn as much as possible.

- Pay attention, ask questions, and participate in classroom activities.
- Practice the things that we learn, and keep up with our assignments.
- Carefully check our work before turning it in. Only turn in work that we are proud of.
- Learn from our classmates and our own mistakes, not just from the teacher.
- Ask for help if we are confused.

RULE 2: Make the classroom a good place for everyone to live and learn in.

- Be quiet when other people are talking or working.
- Treat people and things the way we would want others to treat us and our things.
- Be friendly, respectful, and polite.
- Help our classmates learn.
- Instead of putting people down, put them up! Offer encouragement instead of criticism.

⬤ Teacher Talk

➔ While sharing the responsibility for establishing classroom rules and guidelines with students might seem counterintuitive, it can actually be extremely beneficial. Why? Because students are more committed to guidelines that they have a stake in creating, and they are more likely to comply with guidelines whose purpose they understand.

➔ Don't assume that behavioral guidelines are self-explanatory. Explain and illustrate these guidelines for students at the start of the year using modeling, role-playing, and concrete examples. (Teaching guidelines directly is particularly important at the primary and elementary levels.) Try using charades for reinforcement: ask a student to act out one of the guidelines, let whichever student guesses the guideline correctly act out the next one, and continue on in this manner until all the guidelines have been modeled. Remember that the time you invest in establishing rules and guidelines at the start of the year will pay off later in the form of increased time-on-task and enhanced student achievement.

➔ Don't skip Step 6! Developing effective guidelines is the key to *establishing* a productive learning environment, but reviewing, revising, and enforcing these guidelines throughout the year is the key to *maintaining* that environment.

➔ Use friendly and age-appropriate language when discussing concepts like rules and guidelines. When asking students to generate rule-supporting behaviors in Step 3, for example, you might avoid an unfriendly term like "behavioral guidelines" and ask students to generate a list of "here's hows" instead. ("Here's how we can support each rule…")

➔ Turn your list of rules and guidelines into a "classroom compact" by having students sign their names to the final document (see example below). By signing their names, students indicate their commitment to following the guidelines that they developed as a class.

Student-Friendly Learning Targets

What is it?

A tool that uses specific and student-friendly language to clarify classroom learning expectations

What are the benefits of using this tool?

In every well-managed classroom, teaching and learning are driven by clearly defined outcomes. What are students expected to know and understand? What skills and habits are they working to develop? But having clearly defined learning outcomes isn't good enough. We need to share these outcomes with our students so that students can participate in assessing and managing their own learning. This tool outlines a simple process for crafting learning targets that are both understandable and assessable by students. It also reinforces the idea that learning targets shouldn't be posted at the start of a unit and then forgotten about; rather, they must be revisited and assessed throughout the course of instruction.

What are the basic steps?

1. Generate a list of learning targets for an upcoming lesson or unit. To do this, review the standards you intend to address, and ask yourself what you want students to know, understand, and be able to do by the end of the lesson or unit.

   Tip: Be sure to list targets (what you want students to know, understand, and be able to do) rather than activities (the things students will be doing in class).

2. Make your list of targets student friendly. To do this,
   - Write the targets in an "I will" format. (I will know / understand / be able to _____.)
   - Frame the targets in simple, age-appropriate language that students will understand.
   - Be specific. A well-written target should tell students what they're trying to achieve and let them assess their ability to achieve it.

3. Post the list in a prominent location and leave it there throughout the lesson or unit. Discuss each target with students so they're clear about what they're aiming for and why it's worthwhile. ("We'll be learning how to use a book's index. This is important because . . .")

   Note: Alternative methods of sharing learning targets are discussed in Teacher Talk.

4. Refer to the list regularly to show students how what they're doing in class (tasks, activities, and assignments) relates to what they're supposed to be learning (targets).

   Sample language: Today, you'll be examining *yes* and *no* examples of prime numbers (activity). The goal of this activity is to understand and be able to define what a prime number is (target).

5. Remind students to revisit the list of targets throughout the lesson or unit to gauge their progress.

How is this tool used in the classroom?

✔ To develop relevant and specific learning targets

✔ To clarify classroom learning expectations

✔ To help students assess and monitor their learning

EXAMPLE 1: Here's how one teacher transformed a specific standard from the Common Core State Standards for Mathematics (National Governors Association Center for Best Practices, Council of Chief State School Officers [NGA Center/CCSSO], 2010b) into a set of student-friendly learning targets:

Standard that I intend to address:

4.NF.A.2: Compare two fractions with different numerators and different denominators, e.g., by creating common denominators or numerators, or by comparing to a benchmark fraction such as 1/2. Recognize that comparisons are valid only when the two fractions refer to the same whole. Record the results of comparisons with symbols >, =, or <, and justify the conclusions, e.g., by using a visual fraction model.

Student-friendly learning targets:

- I will be able to define these terms in my own words and give an example of each: *fraction, equivalent fraction, numerator, denominator,* and *value.* I will also be able to explain what it means to *compare* two things.

- I will know what these three symbols mean and how and when to use them: >, =, <.

- I will be able to compare fractions with different numerators and denominators.

- I will be able to tell when fractions are equivalent.

- I will be able to show and explain how fractions can be equivalent even though they may look different.

- I will be able to express fractions using visual models (like pictures or number lines) as well as numbers.

EXAMPLE 2: A high school English teacher developed the list of student-friendly learning targets shown below for a unit on arguments.

Student-friendly learning targets:

- I will be able to define the key components of an argument in my own words: *claim, reasons, evidence, counterclaim,* and *conclusion.*

- I will be able to analyze written arguments and identify their key components.

- I will be able to describe the basic structure and purpose of an argument.

- I will be able to craft a high-quality argument on my own.

- I will be able to explain why making high-quality arguments is a critical 21st century skill.

EXAMPLE 3: A primary-grade teacher makes student-friendly learning targets even more friendly for her young learners by expressing those targets using pictures as well as words (see examples below). She also limits the number of targets that she asks her students to focus on at any one time.

 I will know how to call for help.

 I will know when it's safe to cross the street.

🎯 Teacher Talk

➜ When framing your learning targets in Step 2, keep in mind that the notion of *understanding* can be hard to define and assess. So, instead of writing targets that use the word *understand*, you might consider wording that is more specific. Instead of "I will *understand* how plants make food," for example, you might try "I will be able to *explain* how plants make food."

➜ Learning targets are often introduced at the start of a lesson or unit to guide the learning process, but you can share them at other points in an instructional sequence as well—and in a number of different ways. Instead of *telling* students the targets, for example, you could invite them to uncover the targets for themselves by having them analyze a culminating assessment task ("What will you need to know and be able to do in order to complete this task successfully?") or complete an activity ("What did we learn by creating a plot of temperature versus elevation?"). And instead of simply posting targets on the board, you could use an engaging "hook" or activity to concretize and give context to the targets. ("What's the difference between the subtraction problems we learned to solve yesterday and the new ones on the board? Today, we're going to learn how to use a technique called 'borrowing' to tackle these new problems.")

Ultimately, the time and method you use to share your targets should be determined by the content and purpose of your lesson. Regardless of how and when you share your targets, students should be able to explain what they're supposed to be learning long before that learning is assessed. Check their ability to do this by posing questions like "Why are we doing this?" or "What's our goal?"

➜ Learning targets that are student friendly are also parent friendly. When you describe learning targets using everyday language, you're helping establish a common language that is accessible to all stakeholders, including parents. This common language makes it easier for parents to support their children's learning efforts.

➜ Today's standards-based assessment tests require students to analyze complex tasks and determine what those tasks demand. While this tool doesn't develop students' task analysis skills (because it's the teacher who generates the learning targets), the Backwards Learning tool (Boutz, Silver, Jackson, & Perini, 2012) does.* To use Backwards Learning, teach students to review an assigned task, summarize the task in their own words, and identify knowing and doing goals (learning targets) as outlined below. Early on, students will likely need help conducting this kind of analysis, but over time, they'll develop the ability to analyze tasks more independently.

• Teach students to identify *knowing* goals by asking themselves, "What will I need to know or understand in order to complete this task successfully?"

• Teach students to identify *doing* goals by asking themselves, "What will I need to be able to do in order to complete this task successfully? What skills will I need to master?"

➜ Clarifying behavioral expectations is just as important as clarifying learning expectations. Use the guidelines in Step 2 to help you develop behavioral expectations that are easy for students to understand and follow. Express the behaviors in positive terms (say what students *should* do rather than what they shouldn't), teach them explicitly, and refer to / enforce them throughout the year.

---

*A reproducible visual organizer for the Backwards Learning tool, as well as examples of completed student organizers, can be found at www.ThoughtfulClassroom.com/Tools.

2

Building Positive Relationships

How can I build meaningful relationships with students and among students to promote learning?

Alone we can do so little; together we can do so much.

—Helen Keller

Relationships make a difference in the way students perform in school. They can also make the process of giving students what they need in the classroom a little easier.

—Nina Sears, "Building Relationships with Students"

The second cornerstone of effective classrooms is Positive Relationships, and it is the cornerstone that reminds us that learning is a deeply social act. Building this cornerstone ensures that the classroom operates as a community in which students pursue learning collaboratively, discuss and refine their ideas as equals, resolve conflicts maturely, and in the most general sense, enjoy working together. What's more, building this cornerstone—and the collaborative and interpersonal skills that support it—prepares students for college and career success. Indeed, collaboration and communication/interpersonal skills have been identified as two of the most critical "soft" skills for college- and workplace-bound students to develop (Holmes, 2014).

Of course, learning is more than a social act; it is also highly personal, which is why a second aspect of this cornerstone relates to understanding who our students are and what motivates them. By committing to learning about each student, we show students that we care about them as individuals. And by using what we learn about each student to make learning more personal, we can boost achievement and self-esteem.

This chapter presents six tools that address the social and personal elements of the Positive Relationships cornerstone:

1. **All for One & One for All** helps teachers design cooperative learning experiences that call for high levels of interaction, collaboration, and mutual support among classmates.

2. **Check Your Mood at the Door** prepares teachers to understand and respond to how students are feeling each day by having students assess and describe their mood as they enter the classroom.

3. **Community CIRCLE** uses students' collective knowledge and experiences to drive collaborative conversations around critical content; it ensures that these conversations are productive and respectful by establishing clear rules for participation.

4. **Getting to Know You** promotes effective teaching and positive teacher-student relationships by inviting students to share their interests, talents, learning preferences, and goals.

5. **Interaction in an Instant** presents quick and easy ways to get students talking to and learning from their classmates.

6. **Say "S" to Resolving Conflicts** outlines a simple procedure that students can use to resolve classroom conflicts collaboratively.

All for One & One for All

What is it?

A tool that helps students get more out of cooperative learning experiences by requiring them to work together, support each other, and pull their own weight

What are the benefits of using this tool?

Establishing a collaborative classroom community where students learn both *with* and *from* each other is critical. Cooperative learning activities can help, but putting students into groups and letting them go isn't good enough. In order to be effective, cooperative learning activities need to be structured so that they promote collaboration and combined achievement rather than off-task behavior and freeloading. All for One & One for All presents seven easy-to-use structures that fulfill these critical criteria and engage students in truly cooperative group work.

What are the basic steps?

1. Identify a learning goal or task that is suited to cooperative work. Decide which of the cooperative learning structures on pp. 30–31 is the best fit for your chosen goal or task.

2. Organize students into mixed-ability-level teams of three to six students each. Describe the goal or task you want them to work on and the cooperative structure that you selected. Confirm that students understand their roles and responsibilities within the selected structure.

3. Introduce the principles of individual accountability and positive interdependence (adapted from Johnson & Johnson, 1994) using simple and student-friendly language:

    - *Individual accountability* means that everyone is responsible for doing his or her fair share and for learning and being able to explain all the relevant material.

    - *Positive interdependence* means that you and your teammates are in it together—that you'll need to work together and/or help each other learn in order to be successful.

4. Clarify that effective group work involves both of these principles. Discuss the way that these principles work to promote learning, productivity, and positive relationships among teammates.

5. Observe students as they begin working. Use questions like these to help them assess and improve their performance (their own as well as their team's):
    - How did you decide who would do what? Is this a fair distribution of labor? Why or why not?
    - How are you personally contributing to the success of your team? How are you helping others?
    - Do you understand this material well enough to explain it to someone else?
    - How is your team as a whole ensuring that everyone understands the relevant material?

6. Help students assess and learn from the overall experience by posing reflection questions (e.g., What are some benefits of working collaboratively? How did your team function? What could you do better next time?) or distributing Team-O-Graph forms (see pp. 32–33 for options).

How is this tool used in the classroom?

✔ To make cooperative learning experiences more positive and productive

✔ To establish clear behavioral expectations for cooperative learning experiences

✔ To help students develop collaborative and supportive relationships with their peers

Teachers use the cooperative learning structures that follow to engage students in a range of activities, including reviewing content, researching topics/issues, and solving complex problems.

Seven Cooperative Learning Structures

United We Stand

With this technique, team members demonstrate their learning by producing and submitting a single product (e.g., essay, diorama, skit, lab report) that everyone has contributed to in some way. Students are responsible for deciding who will do what and for dividing tasks fairly. (A brief note explaining the division of labor should be included with the final product.) Students understand that they will receive a shared grade for their work and are responsible for all the relevant material.

To Each His Own

With To Each His Own, team members work together to research, discuss, or practice the assigned material, but ultimately produce their own products. Students understand that their final grades will be a reflection of everyone's work, either an average of all team members' scores *or* the sum of the team average plus their own individual scores (your decision, but tell students in advance).

Note: You can tell students what type of product to create or let them show what they know using any format that appeals to them ("Research the causes/effects of climate change as a team. Then create products—one per person, any type of product you want—that show what you learned").

Divide and Conquer

Here, the materials students need to complete an assigned task, project, or problem are distributed to different team members so that students must work together and share resources in order to be successful. For a map-based measuring task, one student might be given the map, another might be given a centimeter ruler, a third might be given the instructions, and so on. For a document-based essay task, different students might be given different primary documents. For a solve-the-mystery task, one student might be given background information, while the rest receive relevant clues.

Sign Off

In this technique, which is designed to prevent students from sitting back and letting others do the work, every member of the team has to sign off on completed work before submitting it. The trick is that students can only sign off if they agree that every member of the team (1) has contributed to the final product, (2) has encouraged his or her team members to contribute/participate, and (3) grasps the relevant content well enough to present or explain it if called on. Students understand that their work won't be accepted by the teacher until it receives everyone's signature.

Note: Sign Off can be used in combination with other cooperative learning techniques that require team members to produce a single final product or response.

Pick 'Em at Random

Here, students begin by working together to solve a problem, answer a question, or learn about a specific topic/concept. One student from each group is then randomly selected to share the group's response. Students understand that their grade will be determined by the quality of this person's response. Note that numbering group members in advance and calling on numbers rather than names ("Can all the twos stand up and share?") can help keep the selection process random.

Meet, Then Compete

With this technique, students review and practice key content knowledge/skills with members of their "home team." They then compete against members of other teams and bring the points they earn back to their home team. The home team with the highest score at the end is the winner.

The type of competition that students engage in is entirely up to you. Here are two possibilities:

- *Skills Competition:* Pairs of students square off in a "skills competition" (e.g., solving ten math problems or completing twenty conjugation exercises). Students correct their work using a teacher-provided answer sheet and earn points for correct answers. The student with the most points is awarded five "team points" to bring back to his or her home team. The other student is awarded three team points. In the case of a tie, both students receive four points. Offer a one-point bonus for perfect scores.

- *Study Showdown:* Students work with their home teams to review big ideas and important details about a given topic. They list their ideas on "showdown sheets" (one per student), compare sheets with someone from another team, and earn a point for each item their opponent doesn't have. Be sure to moderate the initial idea-generating sessions so that students focus on important-to-know facts and details rather than trivial ones. Because students receive points for ideas their competitors don't have, they might be tempted to record anything and everything—important or not—on their showdown sheets.

Since the goal is to maximize team points, students should use the initial practice session to make sure that everyone on their home team is prepared for competition. To keep the competition fair and confidence high, have students compete against individuals of similar ability levels.

Jigsaw

The Jigsaw strategy (Aronson et al., 1978) builds research and communication skills by having students learn about different aspects of a given topic and then share what they learned with their classmates. Students are broken into three- to five-member Jigsaw teams, and each member of the team is charged with becoming an expert on a different subtopic. If the topic were reptiles, for example, one student might become the "survival expert" (How do different kinds of reptiles defend themselves? What adaptations help them survive?), one might become the "food and habitat expert" (Where do reptiles live? What do they eat? In what kinds of climates do they thrive?), and so on.

Once subtopics have been assigned, students leave their Jigsaw teams to join "expert groups" made up of students from other teams who are researching the same subtopic. These experts work together to research their subtopic, agree on the most important information to collect, and discuss the best method for teaching that information to their original team members. When Jigsaw teams reconvene, students share their knowledge with their teammates and develop some kind of product (chosen by you or them) that reflects their combined expertise. Students understand that they are responsible for understanding all the material, not just the material that they researched.

My name: _____ Date: _____

My team members' names: _____

Activity or assignment: _____

Team-O-Graph, version 1

CRITERIA FOR SUCCESSFUL GROUP WORK	Not Really	Sort of	Yes!
I participated and helped my team succeed.	☹	😐	🙂
Everyone else participated and helped the team succeed.	☹	😐	🙂
I listened quietly when others were speaking.	☹	😐	🙂
Everyone took turns speaking.	☹	😐	🙂
I stayed focused on my work.	☹	😐	🙂
Everyone stayed focused on his or her work.	☹	😐	🙂
We worked well as a team.	☹	😐	🙂

What did I do to help my team succeed?

How could my team have done even better?

My name: _____   Date: _____

My team members' names: _____

Activity or assignment: _____

Team-O-Graph, version 2

Review the criteria for successful group work *before you begin working* on the given assignment or activity. Keep the criteria in mind *as you work*. Use the criteria to rate your own and your entire team's performance *after you finish working*.

CRITERIA FOR SUCCESSFUL GROUP WORK	Not really	Somewhat	Mostly	Definitely
I made a major contribution to my team's success.	1	2	3	4
Everyone else made a major contribution to our success.	1	2	3	4
I stayed on task.	1	2	3	4
Everyone else stayed on task.	1	2	3	4
I learned the required material.	1	2	3	4
Everyone else learned the required material.	1	2	3	4
I sought out help if I needed it, and I accepted help gratefully.	1	2	3	4
Everyone who needed help asked for it and accepted it well.	1	2	3	4
I helped and supported my teammates.	1	2	3	4
All of my teammates helped and supported each other.	1	2	3	4
I gave people feedback about their work, ideas, and progress.	1	2	3	4
Everyone else on the team gave people feedback as well.	1	2	3	4
I treated everyone the way that I'd want to be treated.	1	2	3	4
All of my teammates treated others the way they'd want to be treated.	1	2	3	4

Some things my group did well…

My greatest challenges when working with this group…

Ideas for improvement…

Check Your Mood at the Door

What is it?

A tool that helps us identify issues that might affect student learning by having students assess and describe their moods as they enter the classroom each day*

What are the benefits of using this tool?

Students' moods can change at the drop of a hat. Even the peppiest, most well-behaved student can be brought down by a fight with a friend, a poor performance during a big game, or being grounded. Check Your Mood at the Door provides a quick and easy way to assess students' moods on a day-to-day basis. (Students express how they're feeling using a simple rating scale that's posted near the entrance to the classroom.) The goal is to identify moods that might affect students' behavior or learning capacity, so that we can respond accordingly. Besides preparing us to head off potential problems and teach more effectively, inviting students to tell us how they're feeling each day sends the valuable message that we care about our students as individuals.

What are the basic steps?

1. Develop a three- or four-point scale that students can use to rate their moods as they enter the classroom. Scales can be words only, pictures only, or a blend of words and pictures.

2. Write out your rating scale on large poster paper. Post the scale on the door of your classroom or right near the entrance on a wall or bulletin board.

3. Review the rating scale with your students. Explain that you're interested in knowing how they're feeling each day, and that you'd like them to use the scale to share that information with you when they enter the classroom.

4. Stand near the door when students enter the room each day. Ask students to "hit" the portion of the scale that corresponds to their current mood using a high-five motion.

5. Probe the causes of particularly good, particularly bad, or different-than-usual moods (see sample language below). You can do this either as students enter the room or in a more private setting.

   Sample language: You don't seem your usual upbeat self. Is anything going on? Do you want to share? Can I help you in any way?

   Sample language: You seem particularly happy and excited today. Did something special happen? Is there anything you want to share?

6. Respond to what you learn in Step 5. Look for ways to improve students' moods and/or head off potential behavioral problems. You might, for example, offer a down-in-the-dumps student some words of sympathy, some extra support, or some extra slack in class.

   Tip: Respond to good moods as well as bad ones (e.g., help a student celebrate a happy moment, or capitalize on a student's good mood to get that student engaged and involved in class).

---

*This tool was inspired by the work of our colleague, Beth Knoedelseder.

How is this tool used in the classroom?

✔ To assess and respond to students' moods on a daily basis

✔ To identify and address potential behavioral problems in a proactive way

✔ To convey the message that we care about our students as individuals

EXAMPLE: A middle school teacher found that adding expressive cartoon images to her previously words-only rating scale made the scale easier for students to relate to and more fun for them to use.

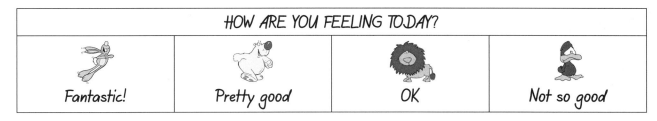

HOW ARE YOU FEELING TODAY?			
Fantastic!	Pretty good	OK	Not so good

🎨 Teacher Talk

➔ If you prefer, you can have students express their moods using descriptive words (e.g., *grumpy, confused, happy*) rather than a rating scale. *Happy Hippo, Angry Duck* (Boynton, 2011) is a great book for introducing younger students to different types of moods and words for describing them.

➔ Pay extra attention to extreme or long-term attitude issues, as they can be signs of bigger-picture or potentially serious problems.

➔ The physical act of hitting the door (or a bulletin board) is fun for many students and can, in and of itself, be a good stress reliever or mood booster. If you'd rather get a snapshot of the entire class's mood at once, give students sticky notes and have them "stick the door" rather than "hit the door."

➔ For variety, invite students to expand on their initial ratings in writing rather than orally. A classroom journal that only you (not students' classmates) will read works well for this purpose.

➔ Discuss the impact that moods can have on students' engagement level, behavior, and academic performance. Teach students that they have the capacity to control and change bad moods, and discuss specific strategies for doing this. Here are some possibilities:

• Talk through problems with someone you trust (e.g., teacher, friend, parent, counselor, coach).

• Do something to get your mind off whatever is bothering you.

• Don't dwell on all the things you need to accomplish; make a to-do list and get started!

• Ask your teacher for help with classroom-specific problems like not understanding the material.

• Focus on the good things in your life rather than the bad ones.

• Talk to yourself using positive and action-oriented language (e.g., "I won't let that person's comments get me down!" or "I can get better at this if I keep practicing").

• Put your problems aside—literally—by writing them on index cards and putting the cards in a box. (*Note:* Students can do this individually or as a class. If you create a class box, periodically pull problems out—don't say who they belong to—and discuss strategies for addressing them.)

Community CIRCLE

What is it?

A discussion technique that encourages students to share their prior knowledge, experiences, and opinions as they explore critical content collaboratively

What are the benefits of using this tool?

Positive relationships are built through conversations. Indeed, when students know how to listen actively when their peers are speaking, when they address their fellow students by name, and when they feel comfortable expressing their own thoughts, the classroom operates as a learning community. Community CIRCLE helps develop this kind of conversational culture, so students can explore critical content collaboratively. What's more, by using students' personal knowledge, experiences, and opinions to drive these collaborative conversations, the tool gets students actively engaged and participating in the learning process.

What are the basic steps?

1. Establish the ground rules for the Community CIRCLE. Explain that all students should come prepared to share, listen carefully to their peers, and use one another's names when they speak.

2. Use the CIRCLE technique to run Community CIRCLE sessions:

Create a question or prompt that invites students to share their personal knowledge, experiences, or opinions about a specific topic.

Invite students to sit in a circle and share their responses. Encourage all students to participate.

Review key ideas by having students summarize each other's responses. Ask students to use their classmates' names when summarizing. ("Gabe said he thought that . . .")

Compare responses. Help students look for similarities and differences among their ideas.

Look for patterns. Help students identify big ideas, make generalizations, and draw conclusions.

Extend the thinking and learning process. You can do this by assigning a synthesis task or connecting Community CIRCLE responses to upcoming learning. ("Let's see how our ideas about friendship compare to those in the next book we'll be reading . . .")

Note: The goal is to have many students share many specific ideas by drawing on their prior knowledge and experiences. Analyzing these specifics, finding commonalities, and developing generalizations then become the collaborative charge of the class.

3. Teach or review positive discussion behaviors (e.g., listening carefully, disagreeing respectfully, asking questions, addressing classmates by name) before initiating a Community CIRCLE. Assess and acknowledge students' use of these behaviors throughout the CIRCLE process.

4. Make Community CIRCLE a regular part of your classroom culture, both by using it consistently and by encouraging students to use the same basic process when working in small groups (i.e., share and review ideas, compare ideas and look for patterns, form generalizations and conclusions).

How is this tool used in the classroom?

✔ To engage students in discussing critical concepts and content collaboratively

✔ To develop a regular and comfortable forum for students to share their ideas and experiences

✔ To help students connect their prior knowledge and experiences to classroom content

✔ To teach and reinforce positive discussion behaviors

EXAMPLE 1: A middle school teacher uses the Community CIRCLE process to help her students discover the relationship between attitude and achievement. Here's what each step looks like:

Create a prompt that invites students to share personal knowledge, experiences, or opinions.

The teacher uses the following prompt to get students thinking about their personal experiences with the attitude/achievement relationship: "Think of a time when your attitude has either helped or gotten in the way of your success. How did your attitude affect your success?" To prepare students for the sharing process, she has them jot down their ideas on paper before joining the circle.

Invite students to sit in a circle and share their responses.

Students arrange their chairs in a circle and begin sharing. Everyone is required to participate.

Review key ideas by having students summarize each other's responses.

Students restate or summarize their classmates' ideas, making sure to refer to each other by name.

Compare responses.

With the teacher's help, students identify similarities and differences like these:

- "Taryn's and Carlos's experiences seem similar. Both spoke about how a coach helped them improve their attitude and how their improved attitude helped them get better at their sport."

- "Joe and Amy had very different opinions. Amy didn't believe that her attitude affected her performance in class, but Joe was convinced that his did. He supported his belief with several specific examples, like how when he made an effort to have a more positive attitude about math, he actually started doing better in math class."

Look for patterns.

The teacher challenges students to develop generalizations about attitude that are rooted in their collective experiences. After some discussion and debate, students agree to these two generalizations: (1) Your attitude can affect your performance; (2) it's better to have a positive attitude than a negative one.

Extend the thinking and learning process.

The teacher asks students to read the classic American poem "Casey at the Bat" and look for evidence that supports and/or refutes their generalizations about attitude.

EXAMPLE 2: A primary-grade teacher uses Community CIRCLE to help students explore and assess the effectiveness of various conflict-resolution strategies. He opens the discussion with the following prompt: "Think of a time when you had a disagreement or fight with someone. What did you do to try and fix the situation?" Next, he helps students compare their individual approaches, discuss pros/cons, and identify the five approaches they think are most effective. To extend and solidify student learning, he has students create a picture book of appropriate ways to resolve a conflict.

EXAMPLE 3: A middle school English teacher uses Community CIRCLE to help students discover some of the strategies that writers use to make their stories engaging. She opens the discussion with this prompt: "Think about some stories or novels that you've really enjoyed reading. Why were these pieces enjoyable to read? What did the author do to capture your interest?" She then helps students compare and look for patterns among their responses. ("We seem to agree that engaging stories have openings that grab your attention, interesting characters, lively dialogue . . .") Finally, she challenges students to extend and apply what they've learned by writing an engaging story of their own that uses at least three of the engaging elements they identified during the discussion.

EXAMPLE 4: A high school history teacher presents this prompt at the end of a unit on World War I: "For what purposes, and under what conditions, should our country deploy its armed forces?" After students share and defend their positions, they work to reach a consensus on some common principles. Over the course of the year, students revisit and refine these principles as they evaluate the United States' decision to participate in other military engagements.

🔘 Teacher Talk

➔ Remember that the goal of Community CIRCLE isn't to have students share for the sake of sharing. It's to use students' personal knowledge, experiences, and opinions as a framework for discussing and learning critical content. For this reason, be sure to have a concrete purpose or learning goal in mind when you initiate a Community CIRCLE conversation. Keep this purpose or goal in mind as you craft your initial prompt, guide the conversation, and develop your synthesis task.

➔ You can promote more interactive and thoughtful conversations by encouraging students to jot down their ideas before joining the circle. Younger students can use pictures rather than words.

➔ Teachers often think that "sharing tools" are just for primary or elementary teachers. Not so! Because Community CIRCLE discussions can be designed around just about any topic, they can work in any classroom. Examples 1–4 and the sample prompts below show how the tool can work across grade levels and content areas.

➔ If you're not sure where to begin, consider prompts that invite students to

- *Explore a critical theme or concept.* For example:
  — What does it mean to be brave?
  — What do scientists do? How do they think and behave? What does it mean to be a scientist?

- *Analyze and/or weigh in on a challenging decision.* For example:
  — Why do you think the mouse decided to leave home? Was his decision a good one?
  — Was President Truman right to use the atomic bomb? Explain your reasoning.

- *Analyze causes and/or effects.* For example:
  — What makes a class engaging? What kinds of classes or teachers get you excited to learn?
  — What if you couldn't use fractions? How might your life be different?

- *Activate and consolidate prior knowledge.* For example:
  — We are about to learn about Lewis and Clark's expedition west. Based on what you know about the United States at this time, what challenges do you believe Lewis and Clark faced?

Getting to Know You

What is it?

A collection of techniques that helps us understand and capitalize on our students' unique personalities by inviting students to share their interests, talents, learning preferences, and goals

What are the benefits of using this tool?

One of the simplest and most powerful statements about good instruction comes from differentiation experts Carol Ann Tomlinson and Marcia Imbeau (2010): "To teach a student well, a teacher must know that student well" (p. 58). Indeed, beginning on the first day of school, effective teachers seek to learn what makes each and every learner tick. What are students interested in outside of school? What inspires them to work hard? What are their hopes and dreams for the future? Getting to Know You presents three techniques that make the process of gathering this sort of information both manageable for teachers and engaging for students. Armed with the knowledge this tool provides, teachers can teach more effectively, motivate hard-to-reach students, and build a classroom culture that celebrates each student's individuality.

What are the basic steps?

1. Review the three Getting to Know You techniques described on pp. 40–41. Select a technique that you feel will be useful to you and enjoyable for your students.

2. Explain the technique and its purpose. ("This technique will help *me* get to know you better and teach you more effectively. It will help *you* learn a little bit about your classmates.")

3. Model your chosen technique using yourself as the subject. If you are using the Hand of Knowledge technique, for example, create your own Hand of Knowledge first. Think aloud as you work so students can see what the process entails.

4. Implement the selected technique in the classroom.

5. Review students' responses to gather information about who students are as individuals—what interests them, how they learn best, what they enjoy doing, etc.

6. Think about how you might use the information you gather to make future learning more productive for the entire class or more personalized for individual learners. Here are a few ideas:

- Design (or let students design) activities and assignments that are aligned with their interests.
- Provide opportunities for students to demonstrate and use their individual talents.
- Explain how classroom content is relevant to students' interests and/or dreams for the future.

7. *Optional:* Help students get to know their classmates by having them share and compare responses or by posting students' responses around the room. If you plan to post or have students share their responses with classmates, notify students in advance and get their permission.

How is this tool used in the classroom?

✔ To learn about students' interests, talents, learning preferences, and goals

✔ To establish a classroom culture that celebrates and accommodates student differences

Teachers use the Getting to Know You techniques that follow to gather a wide range of information about their students. They then use what they learn to develop more personalized and effective instructional plans.

Three Getting to Know You Techniques

Hand of Knowledge

In this technique, students trace their hands on paper and then use the space in the fingers and palm to tell us about their interests, talents, learning preferences, and dreams. (If students' hands don't offer enough writing room, distribute Hand of Knowledge organizers instead; see p. 42.) To create their Hands of Knowledge, students use words and/or pictures to answer these questions:

Pinky finger:	What do you do for fun in your free time?
Ring finger:	What is something you're really good at?
Middle finger:	Think about something interesting that you learned outside of school. What is it? Why is it interesting? How did you learn it?
Index finger:	What word or phrase best describes you as a learner?
Thumb:	When school feels hard or boring, what makes it feel that way? Be specific.
Palm:	What is a dream that you have for your future?

The Hand of Knowledge at the right was created by a third grader. Because this student wasn't the only one to note that she disliked "when the directions are confusing," her teacher made a conscious effort to start explaining task directions more clearly. He also started building more cooperative games and other get-out-of-your-seat activities into his lesson plans in an attempt to capitalize on this student's (and other students') fondness for games/sports like pool and soccer. Sure enough, these activities were a hit!

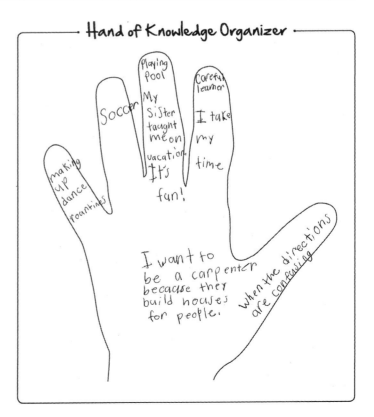

Hand of Knowledge Organizer

Best Foot Forward

Best Foot Forward uses a ten-question survey (p. 43) to help us learn what our students excel at and how we can motivate them. (A high school student's completed survey is shown at the right.) Having this kind of information enables us to develop lesson plans and assessment tasks that take the interests, preferences, and talents of individual students—or the class as a whole—into account.

We might, for example, support this student's preference for clearly stated learning goals and on-point instruction by discussing the relevant learning goals at the start of every lesson and making sure to stay focused on those goals as we teach. To support her preference for work that is challenging but doable, we could use a tool like Graduated Difficulty (Boutz et al., 2012), which presents students with practice tasks at different levels of difficulty and lets them choose the level that's right for them.

> **Best Foot Forward Survey**
>
> 1. I learn best when... my teacher makes it clear what a lesson will be about, I also like an outline.
> 2. My greatest strength is... seeing the big picture and connecting one thing to another
> 3. You'll be happy to have me in your class because... I like to listen to what everyone has to say
> 4. I'm happiest when... my teacher is organized and stays on point and keeps good control of the class.
> 5. A nice thing that a teacher, friend, or family member might say about me is... I am a good listener.
> 6. The subject that I do best in is __English__. Here are some reasons why: I love to read about pretty much anything (except space travel!)
> 7. Things I'm good at outside school include... Mostly I like when we read novels, playing piano, reading
> 8. Things I'm good at in school include... English, French, history extra curricular activities like cheerleading
> 9. If I'm paying attention or working really hard, it's probably because... I want to do well at learning something new - and also because my teacher makes it seem important.
> 10. I do my best work when lessons, activities, and assignments are... challenging but still feel like something I can do.

Letter to My Teacher

Letter to My Teacher asks students to tell us about themselves by writing descriptive letters like the one below. Students are encouraged to share all kinds of information in their letters—personality traits, talents, likes and dislikes, career goals, classroom goals, feelings about school, and so on. (Giving students a list of possible things to write about can often facilitate the process.) Being invited to share this kind of information makes students feel special and valued, and gathering this kind of information helps us better understand, appreciate, and support our students as individuals.

> Dear Mrs. Casey,
>
> My favorite subject is science because I like learning about animals and doing experiments. I also like knowing how and why things work. My goals for this year are to make new friends, not get lost in the school, and learn interesting things. I like playing piano, but I am not very good at it. I am much better at drawing and building things. I also enjoy being outdoors and playing with my dog Minnie. I want to study medicine so I can be a vet and help animals.
>
> I am excited about starting at a new school, but also a little nervous. I hope that people like me and that I do a good job in your class. I promise I will work very hard.
>
> Your friend,
> Katie

Hand of Knowledge

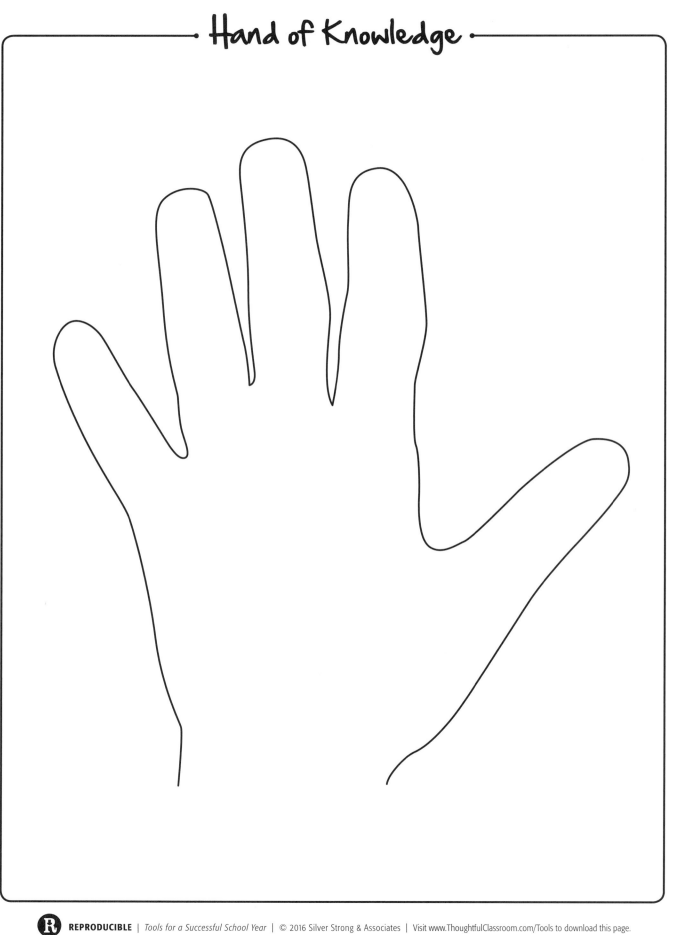

Best Foot Forward Survey

1. I learn best when . . .

2. My greatest strength is . . .

3. You'll be happy to have me in your class because . . .

4. I'm happiest when . . .

5. A nice thing that a teacher, friend, or family member might say about me is . . .

6. The subject that I do best in is _____ . Here are some reasons why:

7. Things I'm good at outside school include . . .

8. Things I'm good at in school include . . .

9. If I'm paying attention or working really hard, it's probably because . . .

10. I do my best work when lessons, activities, and assignments are . . .

Interaction in an Instant

What is it?

A set of pairing and grouping techniques that can be used on the fly to engage students in talking to and learning from their classmates

What are the benefits of using this tool?

Listen to the sounds of students talking in the hallways, in the lunch room, and on the playground, and you'll likely hear lively conversations. What if we could capture a similar level of energy when we ask students to talk about the Crimean War, the respiratory system, percentages—whatever content they're learning in our classrooms? Interaction in an Instant provides four simple-to-implement techniques that promote positive interactions among students. The techniques do more than ask students to talk to one another; they get students engaged in the learning-by-talking process, and they keep students focused on important content. The Interaction in an Instant techniques also help ensure that students talk to and learn from many different students, not just close friends or students who sit near them.

What are the basic steps?

1. Familiarize yourself with the Interaction in an Instant techniques described on pp. 45–46.

2. Select the technique that best meets your instructional objectives.

3. Review the technique with students to make sure they are clear about their roles.

4. Implement the technique in the classroom. Monitor students as they work to ensure that they're staying on task and participating productively.

5. Invite students to share what they learned about the content as well as their reactions to the selected technique.

How is this tool used in the classroom?

✔ To enhance student learning via the use of well-designed pairing and grouping techniques
✔ To foster interaction and collaboration in the classroom
✔ To increase the sense of community among students

Four Interaction in an Instant Techniques

Think-Pair-Share

Think-Pair-Share (Lyman, 1981) allows students to test and refine their ideas with a partner before sharing them with the class or committing them to paper. To use the technique, simply pose a question, prompt, or problem and instruct students to

THINK through a response or solution on their own.

PAIR up with another student to discuss, compare, and refine their ideas.

SHARE their responses with the class or summarize their responses in writing.

Think-Pair-Share is very versatile in the sense that it can be used at any stage of the instructional process (before, during, or after a lesson/unit), and for a variety of different purposes, including activating prior knowledge, reviewing critical content and skills, defining essential attributes, and prompting original or analytical thinking. The sample prompts below reflect these and other uses.

- What do you know about dinosaurs?
- What makes something "art"?
- Was the Civil War inevitable? Why or why not?
- Which of these two math problems is solved incorrectly? How can you tell?
- What do you think the poet was trying to say here? How would you interpret these lines?
- How many ways can you color in exactly half of a ten-by-ten grid?
- What do you predict will happen if we raise the height of this ramp?
- What do you believe were the three most important events in Helen Keller's life? Why?
- What conclusions can you can draw from this data table?

Give One, Get One

Give One, Get One encourages the free flow of ideas and the generation of multiple responses through a rapid series of student-student interactions. Use the technique when you want students to think divergently or come up with many valid responses to a single question/prompt. For example:

- What are the attributes of a good friend?
- Why are plants important to us and our world?
- What are some reasons that people move from one place to another?
- Where are fractions used in the real world?
- What could someone do to improve his or her cardiovascular health?
- Can you name at least seven different styles of music?
- What are some effective strategies for promoting student engagement?

Tell students how many total responses you want them to gather, and give them time to generate two or three on their own. Then, instruct them to meet with another student, *give one* of their responses to their partner, and *get one* in return. Clarify that students shouldn't huddle in groups (pairs only!) or share multiple responses. Instead, they should get only one response from each partner and meet with as many partners as it takes to collect the required number of responses. (If two paired students have identical responses, they should work together to generate a new one.) Conclude by helping students share, summarize, or further explore the responses they collect.

Physical Barometer

Physical Barometer creates instant interactions by requiring students to take positions on multisided issues, discuss and refine those positions with like-minded classmates, and attempt to win over classmates who hold different positions. To use this technique, pose a question or statement that allows students to select from three or more possible positions. For example:

- Where do you stand on the issue of using animals for scientific research? Do you strongly support it, support it, disapprove of it, or strongly disapprove of it?

- We have learned the critical attributes of tall tales, and we have read three different tall tales. Which of the tales we read do you believe would be the best one for teaching a younger student the critical attributes of a tall tale?

- What is your position on the controversy surrounding the proposal to build a "big box" store where the Northvale Farm used to be? Do you support the development of the store, oppose it, or are you not sure?

Once the varying positions that students can take are clear, ask students to go to a physical space that represents their position. For example, the front of the room could represent "support," the back of the room could represent "oppose," and the middle could represent "not sure." Instruct students to work with classmates who share their position to develop and fine-tune a defense of that position. Students in each group should get a chance to make their case and to try to sway members from other groups to change positions and join their group. Students who switch groups should explain what convinced them to change their minds.

Clock Partners

This technique makes the student-pairing process quick and easy, while also ensuring that students don't gravitate to the same learning partners over and over again. To use the technique, distribute copies of the Clock Partners sheet on p. 47 and ask students to "make appointments" with twelve different students—one for each hour on the clock. When two students agree to make an appointment with each other, they must both fill in each other's names on their Clock Partners sheet at the agreed-upon hour. For example, in Zoe's Clock Partners sheet (shown at the right), Zoe made an appointment with Enzo to be her one o'clock partner; consequently, Enzo wrote Zoe in as his one o'clock partner (not shown).

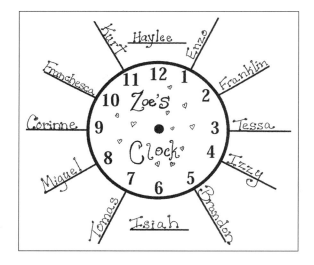

Once students complete their Clock Partners sheets, they can attach their sheets to the inside of their notebooks for safekeeping and ease of access. Then, whenever it comes time for students to pair up, all you need to do is tell them which clock partner to work with, and they can pair up immediately. ("For this activity, you'll be working with your five o'clock partner. Find your partner and get to work!") By rotating around the clock, you can ensure that students work with many different partners instead of always pairing up with the same close friends or neighbors.

Name: _____   Date: _____

Clock Partners

How is this tool used in the classroom?

✔ To teach students a concrete and collaborative procedure for resolving classroom conflicts

✔ To prevent existing conflicts from escalating and future conflicts from occurring

✔ To encourage positive teacher-student and student-student relationships

🎯 Teacher Talk

➜ The first time you use this tool, spend some time discussing what conflicts are, how they affect others, and the importance of resolving them collaboratively.

- Define *conflict* using age-appropriate language. Clarify that conflicts usually begin with some kind of initiating event that has a negative impact on someone else and his or her feelings.

- Use personal examples (or other concrete examples) to help students appreciate the impact that their actions can have on other people's lives and feelings.

- Help students recognize that resolving problems requires all involved parties to participate. A teacher we know helps students come to this realization by asking them to analyze the meaning of this remark from Indira Gandhi (n.d.): "You cannot shake hands with a clenched fist."

➜ Remind students to stick to the facts when describing classroom incidents—and to express how those incidents affect them and make them feel. The idea behind this approach (detailed in Gordon, 1974) is to make "problem-causers" aware of how their behaviors affect others without blaming or judging, since judging and blaming tend to escalate conflicts rather than calm or resolve them.

Tip: Use concrete examples to help students understand what facts-only accounts sound like (e.g., "When you pushed me..." versus "When you acted like a big bully and pushed me...")—and how to express the impact of those incidents without judging or blaming (e.g., "I fell down in front of the whole class and felt embarrassed" versus "You made me fall down and look like an idiot in front of everyone").

➜ Use this tool to address conflicts you have with students, not just conflicts students have with each other. Instead of simply reprimanding a student for yelling out in class, for example, make time to talk the incident through after class. Allowing students to see how their behavior affects you and makes you feel can encourage them to behave more considerately. And showing them that you respect their feelings and are willing to make adjustments on your end ("I'll try to do a better job of noticing when your hand is up") can have a positive impact on teacher-student relationships.

➜ Promote *peaceful* conversations by teaching students strategies for staying calm (e.g., take time to cool off before talking things through, take some deep breaths, or stop periodically to check if you're speaking in calm and quiet tones).

Promote *productive* conversations by preparing students to express themselves effectively. Use concrete prompts (see Step 4) to help students state their ideas clearly, and teach students the vocabulary they need to express their feelings precisely. Creating a word wall of feeling terms (e.g., *angry, betrayed, disappointed, embarrassed, frustrated*) can help.

Promote *self-sufficiency* by teaching students to speak to each other ("You pushed me") rather than to you ("She pushed me")—and look to each other, not to you, for potential solutions.

Say "S" to Resolving Conflicts

STATE WHAT HAPPENED. Stick to the facts.

SHARE CONSEQUENCES, FEELINGS, and MOTIVATIONS. How did the incident affect you? How did it make you feel? Why did you behave or react the way you did?

SEE THE INCIDENT FROM THE OTHER PERSON'S PERSPECTIVE. How might the incident have affected that person? How might it have made him or her feel? Why might he or she have behaved or reacted in that way?

STOP AND DISCUSS your ideas with the other person. Stay calm, keep your cool, and really listen!

SHOW YOU WERE LISTENING. Summarize what the other person said, and acknowledge his or her feelings.

STRATEGIZE TOGETHER. How might you solve the problem or prevent something similar from happening again?

SELECT A FIX-IT STRATEGY that both of you can agree on. Record it here:

SIGN YOUR NAME below to show that you're willing to move past the problem and give your fix-it strategy a try.

3

Increasing Engagement and Enjoyment

How can I motivate students to do their best work and inspire the love of learning?

People rarely succeed at anything unless they have fun doing it.

—Dale Carnegie, *How to Win Friends & Influence People*

Researchers agree that engaged students learn more, retain more, and enjoy learning activities more than students who are not engaged.

—Theresa M. Akey, *School Context, Student Attitudes and Behavior, and Academic Achievement: An Exploratory Analysis*

In surveying a wide body of research on classroom engagement, educational researcher Robert Marzano (2007) concludes that "keeping students engaged is one of the most important considerations for the classroom teacher" (p. 98). This same body of research that Marzano cites tends to define engagement in terms of students' participation, their level of attention, or how on task their behavior is. Clearly participation, attentiveness, and on-task behavior are essential to the success of any classroom, and the tools in this chapter promote such behaviors on the part of students.

But we believe that engagement means more. We believe that the best kind of learning—the kind that that students remember years later—is engaging because it is enjoyable. That's why this cornerstone bears the name Engagement and Enjoyment, and why the tools in this chapter are all designed to make even challenging learning experiences pleasurable for students. More specifically, the tools increase students' motivation to learn by creating variety in the classroom and by tapping natural learning drives, including the drives to excel at classroom learning challenges, compete with fellow students, develop new and original ideas, and strive for "personal bests."

In this chapter, we present six tools that make the classroom more engaging and make learning truly enjoyable:

1. **Classroom Games** provides a variety of adaptable game formats that make reviewing important content fun for students.

2. **Divergent Thinking** offers students a welcome opportunity to think originally and creatively, without fear of being wrong.

3. **Effort Tracker** boosts motivation by helping students recognize that they have the power to improve their academic performance through effort.

4. **Personal Best** helps students feel good about their accomplishments by focusing on forward progress rather than absolute achievement.

5. **Questioning in Style** promotes engagement by infusing variety into classroom questioning sessions.

6. **Scavenger Hunt** makes the process of searching for textual details and evidence more exciting for students by challenging them to go on text-based scavenger hunts.

A final note: Today's increased emphasis on creating learning environments that promote positive behavior (embodied by the growing movement to implement PBIS) means that engagement is more important than ever. Why? Because the best approach to inspiring positive behavior is one that is proactive, one that prevents behavioral issues from occurring in the first place. And working to engage students—to capture their attention and keep them on task—is the very essence of a proactive approach to behavior management. Indeed, an observational study of middle school classrooms found that teachers who used a wide variety of strategies to keep students engaged experienced almost no behavioral problems in the classroom (Raphael, Pressley, & Mohan, 2008).

Classroom Games

What is it?

A tool that presents clear principles for developing engaging and effective classroom games, along with six ready-made game formats to choose from

What are the benefits of using this tool?

Games are fun by definition, which is why many teachers use games to review content. However, not all games are equally effective, and if used poorly, games can amount to little more than a loss of valuable instructional time. On the other hand, well-designed games can help students solidify their grasp of important content and lead to measurable gains in achievement (Haystead & Marzano, 2009). Classroom Games lays out clear design principles for maximizing the power of games in the classroom. It also provides flexible gaming formats that increase motivation, lead to meaningful learning outcomes, and can be applied in nearly any instructional setting.

What are the basic steps?

1. Identify specific content that you want students to review or practice. Decide which of the game formats described on pp. 54–57 will work best with your selected content, or design a game of your own using the CHECKlist of Effective Game Design Principles on p. 58 as a guide.

2. Think through the game in your head to make sure you're clear about how it will work with your content and students. Prepare or gather any necessary materials.

3. Introduce the game by sharing its purpose (e.g., to help students solidify their understanding of key terms from a unit) and explaining the rules and directions.

   Note: If the game includes scoring, outline the scoring procedures, and clarify that scores won't count toward students' grades. (The goal is for students to learn and have fun, not be graded on their performance.) Discuss what good sportsmanship entails, and explain that it's expected.

4. Allow students to play the game. Facilitate as necessary.

5. Help students reflect on and learn from the experience. Ask them what they knew well, what they had trouble with, and what they learned. Encourage them to update and/or revise their classroom notes if needed. ("Did you have that information in your notes? No? Do you want to add it now?")

6. Use students' responses to identify material you might want to review or revisit. ("Lots of students didn't get this; maybe I should reteach it.") Encourage students to do the same. ("Don't waste time studying what you know! Focus on—or ask for help with—the areas that gave you trouble.")

How is this tool used in the classroom?

✔ To make the process of reviewing key content and skills fun and engaging for students

✔ To help students assess their grasp of the targeted material and focus their study accordingly

✔ To help us see what students do and don't know, so we can design instruction accordingly

Six Classroom Game Formats

What's on Your List?

This game format is ideal for reviewing declarative content that fits into categories. To use it, give students a category and challenge them to list as many items in that category as they can within a specified time limit. For example:

- How many Roman gods and goddesses can you name?
- How many types of animal homes can you name?
- How many parts of a cell can you name?
- How many Baroque composers can you name?
- How many map features can you name?
- How many types of polygons can you name?

When time is up, instruct students to compare their lists against a master list that you prepare in advance. Have them award themselves one point for every match. If students generate valid answers that aren't on your list, you can award them bonus points.

To do a more comprehensive review, select a topic with multiple categories and challenge students (or teams of students) to generate as many items as they can in each category. At the end of a unit on World War II, for example, a high school history teacher might break students into three-person teams and present all the teams with the following six categories: *Allied nations*, *Axis nations*, *famous leaders*, *important battles*, *causes behind World War II*, and *new military technology*. Team members would work together to generate as many items as they could in each category and then compare their lists with their teacher's (they'd earn one point for each match). The team with the highest overall point total would be the winner.

Beat the Teacher

This technique uses the power of friendly competition (you versus the class) to help students practice and master important skills. To use it, put a problem on the board (e.g., balance this chemical equation, solve this long division problem), and challenge students to solve the problem at their seats faster than you can solve it at the board. Every student who beats you will earn a point for the class; every time you beat the class, you will earn a point. Award bonus points if students catch errors in your work (intentional ones or inadvertent ones).

Before the competition begins, give students a minute or so to think about the problem and how to solve it. Allow them to review their notes, talk to a neighbor, etc. When time is up, say "Ready, set, GO!" and have everyone start working. Let students know that it's OK to look up at the board and check their work or get ideas from you about how to begin. (Work slowly, so that students have an opportunity to do this—and also to make the competition a bit fairer.) Tell students to put their hands up when they're done. If they beat you, check their answers/work and award "class points" accordingly. Repeat the process with additional problems, increasing the difficulty level as appropriate. Whoever has the most points at the end (you or the class as whole) is the winner.

A & Q

A & Q challenges students to think generatively and get all they know about a given topic out into the open. The game achieves this purpose by reversing the traditional question-and-answer format. Instead of giving students a question and asking them to generate an answer, students are given an answer and asked to generate possible questions that might lead to that answer. If a music history teacher wanted students to review everything they had learned about the Beatles, for example, he might ask, "If 'the Beatles' is the answer, what might the questions be?"—and students might respond with questions like these:

- Who goes by the name "The Fab Four"?
- What band led the "British Invasion"?
- What band recorded the album *Sgt. Pepper's Lonely Hearts Club Band*?
- What band was made up of John Lennon, Paul McCartney, George Harrison, and Ringo Starr?

A & Q can be used in a number of ways:

- In a *shout-it-out session*, you give students answers and challenge them to shout out as many possible questions as they can in a given amount of time.

- In a *head-to-head competition*, teams of students compete against each other to see who can generate the greatest number of legitimate questions to a variety of pre-generated answers. You should serve as judge if the competitors can't agree on the legitimacy of a question.

- In a *station-to-station challenge*, students move around the room—individually or in groups—and record questions for answers that you've written on poster paper. (The challenge is for students to develop answers their classmates haven't already thought of.) Here, for example, are the six posters that a teacher created for a unit on our solar system:

If *Earth* is the answer, what are the possible questions?	If *Mars rover* is the answer, what are the possible questions?	If *orbit* is the answer, what are the possible questions?
If *satellite* is the answer, what are the possible questions?	If the *Milky Way* is the answer, what are the possible questions?	If *solar system* is the answer, what are the possible questions?

Flashlight Fridays

This game format offers a fun way for students to review and practice using critical vocabulary terms. To use it, grab a flashlight, cue up some music, and instruct students to sit facing a classroom word wall. Have students take turns shining a flashlight on the word wall and moving the light around so that various terms are highlighted as the music plays. Every five to twenty seconds, stop the music and instruct the student with the flashlight to freeze. Then, invite multiple students to share their understanding of whatever word is highlighted at the time. Encourage students to show their understanding in different ways. Instead of giving a standard dictionary definition, for example, students might choose to

- Use the highlighted term in a sentence.
- Give a synonym or antonym.
- Define the term using pictures instead of (or in addition to) words.
- Complete a simile about the term. For example, "A *colony* is like a child because …"
- Classify or give an example of the term. For example, "A *pulley* is a type of simple machine."
- Explain how the term fits into the bigger picture or relates to the overall topic of the word wall.
- Explain the connection between two or more highlighted terms from the word wall. (Note that this challenge requires multiple flashlights.)

Challenging different students to define the highlighted terms in different ways is a great way to promote broad participation and depth of understanding. Be sure to correct any misconceptions and help students discuss and refine their responses as a class. Confirm that all students are clear about the meaning of the highlighted term before moving on.

Note: While this game is named Flashlight Fridays because many teachers find that its engaging format keeps students from "checking out early" on Friday afternoons, it obviously works just as well on any other day of the week.

I'm Thinking Of …

This technique helps students review the critical attributes of important people, places, things, and concepts while developing their deductive reasoning skills. To use it, select items from a unit of study and have students pose a series of thoughtfully designed *yes* or *no* questions that will help them identify the selected items. (Students can guess as a class or work in pairs.) Instruct students to frame their questions around critical attributes rather than inconsequential or trivial information, and teach them how to do so. For example, if students are working to identify specific states, you should encourage them to ask attribute-focused questions like "Is the state on the East Coast?" or "Was it one of the original thirteen colonies?" rather than questions like "Does it begin with the letter *M*?," which would help them identify the selected states, but do little to advance or assess their content knowledge.

To turn this game format into a friendly competition, challenge students to see who can identify the topic or item using the fewest questions. With the state-identification challenge described above, for example, you might pair students up, give them a map of the United States to share, and have them select "secret states" for their partners to guess. Each round would be won by the student who used the fewest *yes* and *no* questions to correctly identify his or her partner's state. (To keep the competition as fair as possible, students should be paired with partners of similar ability levels.)

I'm Thinking Of… works especially well with topics like these that contain multiple related examples:

- Geometric shapes
- Animals
- People and places in the community (e.g., mayor, firefighters, municipal buildings)
- Elements on the periodic table
- Instruments in an orchestra
- Organs of the body
- US presidents

Bingo

This game format works just like traditional Bingo, except that the boards are designed around whatever content or skills you're trying to review. Instead of calling out letters and numbers, call out clues or problems such as, "I was the first woman elected to the US Congress." Instruct students to determine the answer, look to see if it's on their board, and mark their boards accordingly. As with traditional Bingo, the first person to mark five spaces in a row (in any direction) is the winner.

You might, for example:

- Test mathematical problem-solving skills by designing Bingo boards with numbers on them, calling out specific problems (e.g., "If I have five teddy bears and I give one to a friend, how many would I have left?"), and having students mark the correct answers on their boards.

- Test students' ability to identify different parts of speech by designing Bingo boards with specific examples on them (e.g., a mixture of nouns, verbs, adjectives, and adverbs), calling out a specific part of speech, and having students mark an appropriate example on their boards.

- Test vocabulary knowledge in a Spanish (or other foreign language) class by designing Bingo boards with Spanish vocabulary words on them, calling out a word in English, and having students mark the Spanish equivalent on their boards.

- Test word knowledge in other content areas by filling Bingo boards with key terms, calling out definitions, and having students mark the corresponding terms on their boards. Another option is to call out words and have students search their boards for synonyms or antonyms.

- Test students' grasp of unit-specific factual knowledge by designing Bingo boards with the names of relevant people, places, and things on them. Pose content-related factual questions (e.g., "Who courageously refused to obey a bus driver's order to give up her seat to a white passenger?"), and have students mark the correct answer on their boards.

While each student's board must be different in order for the game to work—and making those boards can take time—the good news is that once the boards are created, you can use them repeatedly, whether it's later that day, later that week, later that year, or in subsequent years.

Note: To save time, hand the task of creating the boards over to students. Distribute blank five-by-five grids, and tell students what to record in the individual spaces, but allow them to record those items in any spaces they want. You can give students general parameters (e.g., "Fill the boxes with one-digit numbers") or a list of specific items/answers. If you provide a specific list, include more than twenty-five items so that different students' boards will contain different items.

CHECKlist of Effective Game Design Principles*

CHECK to be sure that your game is . . .

Content driven

Don't use games for the sake of using games. Use games to help students review important content or practice relevant skills. Think about what you want students to know or be able to do before designing your game, and then design your game accordingly.

Helpful to you and your students

Well-designed games should give students an opportunity to solidify their understanding of critical content. They should also encourage the kind of reflection and self-assessment that's called for in Step 5 on p. 53. Helping students determine what they do and don't already know prepares them to study in a more focused and efficient way. ("I won't waste time reviewing single-digit addition since I got those problems right during the game. Instead, I'll focus on two-digit addition.") Making this same kind of determination yourself (who needs help with what?) is equally valuable, as it allows you to target instruction accordingly. Depending on what you learn, you might choose to review problematic material with individual students, groups of students, or the entire class.

Engaging

An easy way to make games engaging is to incorporate known "motivational levers" like these:

- *Challenge:* "Can your team identify ten prime numbers in thirty seconds?"
- *Competition:* "Let's see which team is ready to be crowned the Masters of Mitosis and Meiosis!"
- *Choice:* "Which category of question would your team like to select?"
- *Cooperation:* "Before the competition begins, work with your teammates to review your notes and help each other master the material."

Challenging

Games get people excited by challenging them to excel, either individually (think crossword puzzles or Sudoku) or when competing against others (think baseball or Monopoly). When designing games for the classroom, be sure that the challenges are appropriate (not so hard that students give up, not so easy that they're a waste of time) and the competition is inconsequential (students' scores shouldn't count toward classroom grades).

Note: While challenge and competition are natural motivators, competition that causes high levels of anxiety (or causes losing teams or individuals to feel dejected, guilty, or embarrassed) should be avoided. Thus, when designing games that feature competition, be sure to highlight the fun and the learning, not the winning—and give all students an equal opportunity to experience success. To accomplish this goal, Marzano (2007) suggests organizing students into heterogeneous teams (such that low achievers are grouped with high achievers) and restructuring the teams regularly, so that over time, all students are likely to end up on winning teams. Another way to help everyone experience success is to ensure that students compete against students of similar ability levels.

Kindly played

Insist on a gaming environment in which students encourage and help each other, root for each other, and understand how to win and lose with grace. Explain and model good sportsmanship, and call attention to students who exhibit good sportsmanship during competition. Be specific when offering praise so that students understand what they've done well. For example, "I really liked how you shouted out encouraging words to your teammates" instead of "Good job!"

---

*In developing this checklist, we drew on Marzano's (2010) analysis of effective game design principles as well as on our own work and experience helping teachers promote student engagement in the classroom (Silver & Perini, 2010b).

🔘 Teacher Talk

→ There are many tried-and-true game formats that you can use to make reviewing key content engaging, including television game show formats like *Jeopardy!* and *Who Wants to Be a Millionaire?* Choose the formats you are most passionate about, and adapt them to your classroom objectives. Odds are, your passion for the games you select will rub off on your students.

→ If your game uses scoring, be careful. You don't want a winner-takes-all mentality to prevail in the classroom. Think beyond traditional scoring procedures that reward winners and can alienate or embarrass losers. Options to consider include

- Scale-based scoring, in which recognition and/or awards are based on a scale (e.g., 1–5 points gets one prize, 6–10 points gets two prizes, and 11 or more points gets three prizes)

- Bonus scoring, in which students can earn points outside the basic scoring structure (e.g., points for the most creative answer, points for improvement over a previous score, points for exceptional sportsmanship)

- Evil Empire scoring, which involves issuing a challenge like this: "Last year's class got a total of 107 points when we played this game. Let's see if, as a class, we can beat last year's students!"

Divergent Thinking

What is it?

A tool that invites the kind of original and creative thinking that's both exciting for students and highly valued in today's job market

What are the benefits of using this tool?

With all the content we need to cover, making time to encourage open-ended and flexible thinking may not seem like it should be a top priority. But it should. For one, inviting students to think divergently helps them develop a style of thinking that characterizes our most successful innovators and problem solvers—and that's in increasingly high demand in today's job market. Divergent thinking activities are also highly engaging, offering students a welcome change of pace from traditional classroom questioning sessions by inviting them to generate many possible ideas rather than correct answers.

What are the basic steps?

1. Develop a divergent thinking question (see p. 62 for guidance and examples) and present it to students. Explain that the goal isn't to come up with a "right answer" but rather to generate as many different and unique responses as possible.

2. Discuss the criteria you'll use to guide and assess students' progress during the idea-generating stage. The criteria that follow are influenced by Guilford's (1950) ideas on creativity:
   - *Fluency:* Are students generating a lot of responses?
   - *Flexibility:* Are students generating different types or categories of responses?
   - *Originality:* Are students coming up with unique and imaginative responses? Are their responses new and different from existing or expected ones?

3. Invite students to start sharing their ideas, and assess their performance using the criteria above. Use probing and extending questions (see Teacher Talk for ideas) to help students generate more—and more varied—responses.

4. Encourage outside-the-box thinking. ("Stretch your brains! Don't be afraid to come up with ideas that seem crazy or different than everyone else's. Crazy ideas are often the best ideas.") Instruct students not to worry about or judge response quality at this stage; that will come later in Step 5.

5. Help students evaluate the quality of the responses they generate. Guide the process by identifying—or helping students identify—appropriate evaluative criteria. ("How should we decide which are our best ideas? What criteria does it make sense for us to consider?")

   Note: You can use one of the criteria from Step 2 (e.g., "Which is our most *original* response?") or develop criteria that fit your initial question. If students were asked how to solve the school's litter problem, for example, they might judge their ideas based on *feasibility* and *cost-effectiveness*.

How is this tool used in the classroom?

✔ To develop students' ability to think divergently

✔ To make classroom questioning more fun by inviting free thinking rather than "right" answers

✔ To establish a classroom culture where original thinking and creative learners are valued

Teachers use divergent thinking questions to help students develop creative thinking and problem-solving skills. These questions often reflect classroom content (see Example 2 and the sample questions on p. 62), but they don't have to. If the goal is to develop divergent thinking as a stand-alone skill, almost any question that invites multiple creative responses will do (see Example 1).

EXAMPLE 1: Developing divergent thinking as a stand-alone skill

A teacher invited students to think divergently by challenging them to think of as many uses for a pencil as they could. After writing their first five responses on the board (to do schoolwork, to take notes, to solve problems in math class, to do my homework, to do a crossword puzzle), he stopped to provide some formative feedback. First, he pointed out the positives—that students were elaborating on each other's ideas ("By taking the 'doing schoolwork' idea one step further, you were able to create several new responses") and exhibiting *fluency* ("You've come up with five separate answers already"). Next, he used guiding questions (see sample dialogue below) to help students assess their success with regard to *flexibility* and *originality* and to get them going in the right direction.

Teacher:	Do any of the ideas that you've come up with so far seem really creative, different, or original?
Student:	Not really because almost all of them are about writing down stuff for school.
Teacher:	That's a really good point! How many of the answers that you've come up with so far have to do with using a pencil for the purpose of writing something down?
Student:	All of them, actually.
Teacher:	Correct! So … while it's true that you came up with five different answers, you only came up with one kind (or category) of answer. So what does that mean in terms of how *flexibly* you're thinking?
Student:	Not very flexibly.
Teacher:	Let's try to break out of our writing-implement rut and go in a different direction. Anyone?
Student:	This is kind of crazy, but when I was younger, I built a log cabin out of pencils and glue.
Teacher:	Remember that crazy answers are sometimes the best ones! And your answer is definitely *original*. Can someone tell me if the log cabin answer is showing *flexible* thinking, too?
Student:	Yes, because it's a totally different kind of answer than our answers from before. The pencils aren't being used for writing—they are being used to build something.
Teacher:	Great! So can anyone think of another way to use pencils as a building material? Or maybe come up with a different kind of answer in another category completely?

EXAMPLE 2: Developing divergent thinking questions around classroom content

A primary-grade teacher uses this tool during story time. To invite divergent thinking, she stops mid-story to have students generate possible solutions to problems that characters are facing. ("How do you think Frog and Toad might try to solve their cookie-eating problem?") She then challenges students to compare their proposed solutions to the actual solutions in the stories. She's found that asking students to make and test predictions boosts their level of attention and engagement as she reads to them.

Developing Divergent Thinking Questions

To promote divergent thinking, generate questions that can be answered in a variety of ways and that require original thinking as opposed to recall. (Asking students to generate possible solutions to a school's litter problem, for example, would only count as a divergent thinking question if you hadn't already discussed those possibilities as a class.) Among other things, you might invite students to imagine consequences, create associations, generate alternatives, propose improvements, devise explanations, apply information to new contexts, see possibilities, or identify patterns/similarities.

Here are some question stems to get you started:

- How many ways can you _____? Can you think of any other ways to _____?
- What comes to mind when you think of _____?
- How is a _____ like a _____? What is a good metaphor for _____?
- How many ways can you group these words/items/ideas/images/quotations into categories?
- Think about the text you just read. How else might it have ended (or begun)?
- What symbols or icons could you use to represent _____?
- What if _____? What might happen or be different if _____?
- How could you redesign or improve _____? What might be a better way to _____?
- When or how could you use _____?
- Can you generate some possible solutions/strategies/endings/beginnings for _____?
- How could you apply _____ to _____?
- How could you test the hypothesis that _____?
- What are some possible explanations for _____? Why might _____?
- What are some similarities and/or differences between _____ and _____?
- What would be a good title/headline/caption for this story/article/image?
- What might be the meaning of _____? What are some interpretations of/for _____?

Here are some sample questions from different content areas and grade levels:

- How many ways can you use the numbers from 1 to 20 to create an equation that equals 10?
- How many ways can you move from one side of this mat to the other?
- How might we represent this data visually?
- What words, images, or ideas come to mind when you hear the word *prejudice*?
- How is the Brooklyn Bridge like an eagle?
- What if there were no seasons?
- How might history have been different if the United States had joined the League of Nations?
- How could you rewrite this computer algorithm to make it execute more quickly?
- What features might you add to a traditional car interior to increase customer interest?
- What could we do to make this classroom a better place for everyone to live and learn in?
- What are some possible solutions to Junie B. Jones's problem?
- Can you develop some creative strategies for getting kids to eat their vegetables?
- Why might we have gotten a different experimental result than we expected?

⬤ Teacher Talk

➔ Use probing and extending questions to enhance the quality and scope of students' responses in Step 3. Suggestions and sample language are presented below. Additional sample language can be found in Example 1.

- *Actively elicit more ideas:* "Who has another idea to add?"

- *Encourage students to build off each other's ideas:* "Michael thought that rearranging our desks into clusters might encourage more collaboration. Can we explore his room-rearrangement idea a little more? Does anyone have another idea about how we could rearrange our classroom furniture to promote higher levels of collaboration?"

- *Facilitate shifts in student thinking:* "What if we shifted our thinking to consider the causes of pollution and not just the effects? Would that lead us to any new ideas?"

- *Break students out of thinking ruts:* "I notice that all our proposed solutions are fairly similar. Can we stretch our minds and generate some truly creative solutions? Who can come up with an idea that's nothing like the ones we've listed on the board?"

- *Encourage self-assessment:* "How flexibly are we thinking? How many of our solutions to the school's littering problem involve adding more trash containers?"

➔ Highly creative students are often bored and uninspired by conventional convergent-thinking activities, and they may tune out—or act out—as a result. Divergent thinking activities can get these learners excited, motivated, and back on track by giving them a productive outlet for their creativity. Note that students who aren't naturally creative benefit from divergent thinking activities as well, since divergent thinking skills can be improved with guidance and practice.

➔ Classroom activities that allow students to share ideas without fear of being wrong or "looking stupid" are naturally motivating. You can provide an added engagement boost by building in an element of fun and friendly competition. With this tool, for example, you might challenge students—or teams of students—to outthink each other in terms of the number and/or originality of their responses.

➔ Students who prefer to think originally and creatively are at higher risk for academic and attitude/engagement issues than many of their classmates (Hanson, Dewing, Silver, & Strong, 1991). For this reason, it's imperative that we do more to engage and support this group of students in our classrooms. This tool helps us achieve this goal, both by allowing these students to think in a way that appeals to them and by teaching them that the ability to think originally is a valuable ability to possess.

➔ The ability to generate and evaluate novel solutions to important problems is highly valued in the fields of science, engineering, and mathematics; see, for example, Practice 6 from the Next Generation Science Standards (NGSS Lead States, 2013). However, this ability is valued far more broadly as well. Professionals in a wide variety of fields—for example, teaching, consulting, law enforcement, and politics—are tasked with generating and evaluating solutions to problems on a daily basis.

Effort Tracker

What is it?

A tool that motivates students to do their best work by helping them recognize the connection between effort and achievement

What are the benefits of using this tool?

If we expect students to become actively engaged in learning—and to remain engaged when learning becomes difficult—then we must help them cultivate a "growth mindset" (Dweck, 2007a). A growth mindset is the belief that ability and achievement are not fixed but rather that they can be improved through effort, a willingness to try new strategies, and openness to help from others. Effort Tracker is an ideal tool for helping every student develop a growth mindset. The tool invites students to explore the way that effort affects performance, and it uses concrete examples to show students that effort really does matter. Teaching students that they have the power to improve their academic performance is an extremely valuable lesson—one that can increase their motivation, encourage them to persevere in the face of challenges, and enable them to achieve at higher levels (Alderman, 2008; Dweck, 1975, 2007b).

What are the basic steps?

1. Initiate a conversation about the relationship between effort and achievement. Specifically,

   - Use personal, fictional, or real-world examples to illustrate and reinforce the effort/achievement relationship; see Teacher Talk for ideas. Then encourage students to share their own examples.

   - Ask students what effort looks like in a classroom setting. (Is it always giving 100 percent? Asking for help if you're stuck? Proofreading work before turning it in?) Record their ideas on the board.

2. Help students understand that effort involves more than spending time working. Teach them to consider these five criteria (adapted from Moss & Brookhart, 2009) when assessing their performance on an assigned task:

   - *Degree of effort:* How hard did you concentrate or try?
   - *Time spent:* How much time did you spend on this task?
   - *Level of care:* How carefully did you check and correct your work?
   - *Willingness to seek help:* Did you ask questions or seek help if you were stuck or confused?
   - *Use of strategies:* What (if any) strategies did you use while working on this task?

3. Give students a task to work on (e.g., review for a test or make three consecutive free throws).

4. Prepare students to work productively by introducing or reviewing specific strategies that can help them (strategies for writing a focused paragraph, what-to-do-when-stuck strategies, etc.).

5. Have students rate their effort using an Effort Tracker Form (p. 67, Questions 1–5) before submitting their work. Have them reflect on the effort/outcome link after seeing their graded work.

6. Talk to students whose achievement level doesn't reflect their effort level. Help them identify possible reasons for the discrepancy by posing probing questions like these: What do you mean when you say that you worked hard? Did you use any of the strategies that we discussed?

How is this tool used in the classroom?

✔ To have students reflect on and learn from their classroom experiences

✔ To boost motivation by helping students see the link between effort and achievement

EXAMPLE: The form below was completed by a fourth grader.

EFFORT TRACKER FORM

Name: Sally

Assignment: I was asked to write a book review on Charlotte's Web by E. B. White.

---

1) How hard did I concentrate or try?

0 (not at all)   5 (somewhat)   ☆   10 (as hard as I could)

Explanation:

I really liked the book and wanted to do a good job so I worked very hard.

---

2) How much time did I spend studying, practicing, or working on this assignment?

0 (none)   5 (a fair amount)   ☆ 10 (a lot)

Explanation:

I learned how to write a book report last year but I have never written a book review before so I spent a lot of time looking at examples of book reviews so that I would know how to write a good one. I learned a lot by doing that but it still took me a lot of time to write the review because it was something new for me. But I like trying new things so I didn't mind.

---

3) How carefully did I check and correct my work?

0 (not at all)   ☆   5 (somewhat)   10 (extremely)

Explanation:

I spent so much time looking at the sample book reviews and writing my own book review that I hardly had any time left over to proofread my work. I hope that I didn't make too many mistakes.

---

4) Did I ask questions or request help if I was confused?   Yes ☒   No ☐   I didn't need help ☐

5) Which (if any) strategies did I use? I looked at examples of A⁺ work to try and learn from them.

REFLECTION: Did my actions (strategies used + amount of effort) affect my success?   Yes ☒   No ☐

My teacher said that I did an excellent job for someone who had never written a book review before. I don't think that I could've done such a good job if I hadn't looked at the sample book reviews, so looking at examples of other people's work turned out to be a good strategy that was worth my time. My grade for grammar and mechanics isn't very good, but I think it is because I didn't spend enough time proofreading. If I spend more time checking my work, I bet I could do better.

SOURCE: From *Tools for Thoughtful Assessment* (p. 228), by A. L. Boutz, H. F. Silver, J. W. Jackson, and M. J. Perini, 2012, Franklin Lakes, NJ: Thoughtful Education Press. © 2012 by Silver Strong & Associates. Reprinted with permission.

🌐 Teacher Talk

→ Seeing concrete examples helps students recognize that their actions and attitudes can actually influence their level of success. The examples that you present in Step 1 can be personal, real world, or fictional:

- *Personal:* Share stories from your own life. (What have you been able to accomplish by working hard? What disappointments or failures do you owe to a lack of effort rather than a lack of ability?)

- *Real world:* Discuss famous individuals (athletes, politicians, scientists, artists, actors) whose work ethic, determination, and perseverance in the face of setbacks enabled them to succeed. Alternatively, identify individuals whose lack of effort prevented them from achieving their full potential.

- *Fictional:* Use familiar stories to illustrate the idea that effort can be more valuable than innate ability (try "The Tortoise and the Hare") or that working hard and believing in yourself can impact your success (try *The Little Engine That Could*).

→ To use this tool with younger students, simplify the reproducible form as needed. Among other things, you can replace the number lines with smiley faces and frowny faces as shown here:

→ Head off disappointment by having a discussion about realistic expectations *before* returning graded work. Remind students that hard work won't guarantee them a perfect score and that success takes time and sustained effort. Use concrete examples to reinforce this point.

→ To encourage regular self-assessment, you can have students complete Effort Tracker Forms on a daily basis (all but the reflection section) rather than just at the end.

Name: _____ Date: _____

Assignment: _____

Effort Tracker Form

1) How hard did I concentrate or try?

|⊢————————————————+————————————————⊣|
0 (not at all)   5 (somewhat)   10 (as hard as I could)

Explanation:

2) How much time did I spend studying, practicing, or working on this assignment?

|⊢————————————————+————————————————⊣|
0 (none)   5 (a fair amount)   10 (a lot)

Explanation:

3) How carefully did I check and correct my work?

|⊢————————————————+————————————————⊣|
0 (not at all)   5 (somewhat)   10 (extremely)

Explanation:

4) Did I ask questions or request help if I was confused?   Yes ☐   No ☐   I didn't need help ☐

5) Which (if any) strategies did I use?

REFLECTION: Did my actions (strategies used + amount of effort) affect my success?   Yes ☐   No ☐
Explain your answer on the back of this worksheet and/or share your ideas with the class.

Personal Best

What is it?

A tool that motivates students to master new skills by challenging them to improve their performance over time (achieve "personal bests") and helping them visualize their forward progress

What are the benefits of using this tool?

All across the country, track athletes train hard, day in and day out. Many have no expectation of winning their races. What drives these athletes is the deep sense of satisfaction that comes from seeing their efforts pay off as their times improve. Each race becomes a chance to achieve a personal best. This tool taps into the motivational power of the personal best by encouraging students to do their best work and celebrate their achievements. Even more important, it builds the self-assessment skills students need to achieve personal bests by teaching them how to reflect on their work, identify how it has improved, and determine how it can be improved further.

What are the basic steps?

1. Select a skill that you'll be helping students develop over time (e.g., writing the letters of the alphabet, preparing a lab report, crafting a persuasive essay).

2. Give each student a folder labeled with the name of the skill and the words "personal best." Tell students that they'll use these folders to store their work as they practice the selected skill.

   Note: Students' folders can be traditional paper folders or computer folders / e-portfolios.

3. Begin teaching the selected skill, and have students put their first sample of work into their folders. Depending on the skill, this sample could be anything from a problem set to a paragraph to a painting to a status report ("Today, I hit the target with three of my ten pass attempts").

4. Let students know that you'll continue to teach this skill and that they'll continue to practice it. Explain that the goal is for them to get better each time (i.e., to achieve personal bests).

5. Have students add to their folders over time—daily, weekly, or monthly, depending on the skill. Remind them to date all samples of work.

6. Help students compare their current work with their previous work to see how they're improving (e.g., Are their topic sentences stronger and better supported? Are they making fewer errors?).

7. Use the reflection worksheet on p. 69 to help students assess and celebrate their progress and develop plans for future improvements. (Ideally, students should store these worksheets in their folders along with their work.) Discuss or comment on students' work and worksheets as needed.

How is this tool used in the classroom?

✔ To help students evaluate their work and develop plans for improving it

✔ To boost motivation by challenging students to achieve personal bests

✔ To encourage forward progress by helping students see and celebrate their accomplishments

Name: _____ Date: _____

The skill that I am working on is: _____

· Reflecting On My Personal Bests ·

DIRECTIONS: Use the writing prompts below to help you reflect on your progress and make plans for improvement.

I am proud of this work because it is better than my previous work. Here is how it is better...

One reason why the quality of my work has improved is...

Something about my work that I would like to improve further is...

Something that my teacher or a classmate thinks I should work on is...

Note: Only complete this section if you have time to discuss your work with your teacher or a classmate.

My goal for next time is to...

Questioning in Style

What is it?

A questioning technique that uses four different styles of questions to deepen and test students' thinking about critical content—and keep students actively engaged during instruction

What are the benefits of using this tool?

Keeping students engaged throughout the year means avoiding falling into ruts, like asking the same kinds of questions over and over again. But creating the kind of variety that promotes yearlong interest without sacrificing rigor or deep learning can be a real challenge. This tool helps us broaden our questioning repertoires by identifying four distinct styles of questions that we can pose in our classrooms. Besides keeping things fresh and interesting, building different styles of questions into our everyday instruction helps students understand content more deeply (because they explore it from multiple angles) and become more flexible, well-rounded thinkers. Posing different styles of questions is also a great way to assess students' grasp of critical content since no one style of question can give us a complete picture of what students know and understand.

What are the basic steps?

1. Familiarize yourself with the four different styles of questions described below.

   MASTERY questions ask students to *remember* (facts, formulas, definitions, procedures).

   UNDERSTANDING questions ask students to *reason* (analyze, explain, justify with evidence).

   SELF-EXPRESSIVE questions ask students to *create* (similes, predictions, solutions, alternatives).

   INTERPERSONAL questions ask students to *relate* (connect with the content on a personal level).

2. Familiarize students with the four different styles of questions. Explain that each type of question will require them to use a different but equally valuable style of thinking.

3. Generate all four styles of questions about a topic or text you plan to teach (use the Question Stem Menu on p. 72 as a reference). Use the planning form on p. 73 to record your questions.

4. Pose some or all of these questions during an upcoming lesson. Give students time to think before asking for responses. Adjust instruction as needed based on the responses you receive.

   Note: It's important to get all students (not just the usual hand-raisers) engaged in thinking about and responding to classroom questions. One way to achieve this goal is to have everyone jot down a response on paper before inviting anyone to share.

5. Survey students at the end of the lesson to determine which styles of questions (remembering reasoning, creating, relating) they're most and least comfortable answering. Help them develop the skills they'll need to answer all four styles of questions successfully.

   Optional: Use the Introduction to Questions in Style handout (www.ThoughtfulClassroom.com/Tools) to help familiarize students with the different styles of questions and how to respond to them.

How is this tool used in the classroom?

✔ To promote engagement by infusing variety into classroom questioning sessions

✔ To assess student learning in real time and adjust instruction accordingly

✔ To help students become more flexible and well-rounded thinkers

Teachers in all grade levels and content areas use this tool to build different styles of questions into their lessons. Two sets of questions are shown below, and an additional set is available for download at www.ThoughtfulClassroom.com/Tools. (The words that tip you off to each question's style have been italicized for your reference.)

EXAMPLE 1: A first-grade teacher poses different styles of questions during story time to keep her students engaged, check their understanding of what she's read, and target specific reading standards. The questions that she developed for William Steig's *Sylvester and the Magic Pebble* are shown below.

MASTERY QUESTIONS	INTERPERSONAL QUESTIONS
• William Steig is the author and illustrator of this book. *What* does an author do? *What* does an illustrator do? • Can you *retell* what happened so far in your own words?	• *How would you feel* if you were turned into a rock? • How do you think Sylvester's parents are *feeling* in this picture? How can you tell?
UNDERSTANDING QUESTIONS	**SELF-EXPRESSIVE QUESTIONS**
• Is this story more happy or more sad? *Give a reason why* you think so. • Do Sylvester's parents love him? *Explain* how you can tell. Can you *find a specific example* from the book?	• What do you *predict* Sylvester will wish for? • *Can you think of another* (better) wish that Sylvester could have made to escape from the lion?

SOURCE: Adapted from *Tools for Thoughtful Assessment* (p. 68), by A. L. Boutz, H. F. Silver, J. W. Jackson, and M. J. Perini, 2012, Franklin Lakes, NJ: Thoughtful Education Press. © 2012 by Silver Strong & Associates. Adapted with permission.

EXAMPLE 2: Before every lecture, a world history teacher maps out different styles of questions that he can use to check for understanding while teaching. One of his question maps is shown here:

MASTERY QUESTIONS	INTERPERSONAL QUESTIONS
• What is a city-state? *Define* the term and give some examples. • Can you *locate* Sparta on a map? How about Athens? • *Describe* key geographical features of Athens and Sparta.	• Would *you* rather have lived in Athens or Sparta? Would *you feel* the same if you were in *someone else's shoes* (e.g., if you were female, poor, or a slave)? *Share your feelings.* • What do *you* admire about each city-state? Describe an accomplishment, value/belief, institution, etc. • Do *you* see any value in learning about these city-states?
UNDERSTANDING QUESTIONS	**SELF-EXPRESSIVE QUESTIONS**
• *Agree or disagree:* Geography plays a critical role in shaping civilizations. *Give examples* from this or other units. • Does Athens deserve its reputation as the superior city-state? What *evidence* points to yes? What argues no? • How did Athens and Sparta *compare* with regard to views on government, education, the arts, women's rights, etc.?	• *If* one of Athens or Sparta's key geographical features had been different, *how might* the city-state have been different? Pick any feature you want and *speculate.* • Would Sparta have been just as successful *if* it had been a democracy instead of an oligarchy? • Can you *create an original* nickname, motto, or symbol for either city-state that captures the essence of that state?

SOURCE: From *Tools for Thoughtful Assessment* (p. 68), by A. L. Boutz, H. F. Silver, J. W. Jackson, and M. J. Perini, 2012, Franklin Lakes, NJ: Thoughtful Education Press. © 2012 by Silver Strong & Associates. Reprinted with permission.

Question Stem Menu: Four Different Styles of Questions

MASTERY QUESTIONS
ask students to *remember facts and procedures:*

✓ Recall facts and formulas

✓ Observe and describe

✓ Locate, organize, or sequence

✓ Perform procedures/calculations with accuracy

✓ Define, restate, or summarize

Sample question stems:

- Who? What? When? Where?
- What do you know or remember about __?
- Can you list the key points/facts/details from __?
- What did you see, hear, smell, taste, do?
- What are the characteristics or properties of __?
- Can you put these __ in order based on __?
- What happened first? Second? Third?
- Can you show me how to __?
- Can you describe the formula/procedure for __?
- Can you define, retell, or restate __?
- Can you locate or give an example of __?
- Can you calculate __?

INTERPERSONAL QUESTIONS
ask students to *relate on a personal level:*

✓ Share their feelings, reactions, and opinions

✓ Draw connections to their own lives

✓ Assist or advise other people

✓ Put themselves in someone else's shoes

✓ Consider personal preferences and values

Sample question stems:

- How did you feel about __? React to __?
- Where do you stand on __?
- What do you think of __'s choice?
- What was most/least __ (interesting, difficult, etc.)?
- How is __ relevant to your own life? To society?
- Have you experienced something like __ before?
- How could you explain __ to someone else?
- How would you advise this person or character?
- How might this look from the perspective of __?
- If you were this person or character, how would you feel? What would you do?
- Which of these __ is most important to you?

UNDERSTANDING QUESTIONS
ask students to *reason, analyze, and explain:*

✓ Compare and contrast

✓ Explain, reason, or understand why or how

✓ Give reasons, evidence, and examples

✓ Analyze, interpret, evaluate, or conclude

✓ Classify or categorize

Sample question stems:

- What are the key similarities and/or differences?
- Are __ and __ more similar or different? Why?
- What are the causes and/or effects of __?
- Why __? What is the reason for __? Explain.
- How would you support, prove, or disprove __?
- Do you agree or disagree with __? Why?
- Does __ make sense? Explain your reasoning.
- Do you see any flaws or inconsistencies in __?
- What do you think __ means? Why?
- What can you conclude or infer from __?
- What are the central ideas or themes?
- What connections or patterns do you see?
- What larger category/concept does __ belong to?

SELF-EXPRESSIVE QUESTIONS
ask students to *create and explore possibilities:*

✓ Speculate (what if?), hypothesize, or predict

✓ Generate and explore alternatives

✓ Create or design something original

✓ Represent concepts visually/symbolically

✓ Develop and explore similes

Sample question stems:

- What if __? What might happen if __?
- How might __?
- Can you make a prediction about __?
- How many ways can you __?
- Can you think of another __ (explanation, solution, ending, strategy, hypothesis)?
- What other perspectives should we consider?
- Can you create or invent an original __?
- Can you put these __ together in a unique way?
- Can you devise a plan/procedure to __?
- What comes to mind when you think of __?
- How can you represent __ visually or symbolically?
- How is __ like a __?

SOURCE: Adapted from *Tools for Thoughtful Assessment* (p. 69), by A. L. Boutz, H. F. Silver, J. W. Jackson, and M. J. Perini, 2012, Franklin Lakes, NJ: Thoughtful Education Press. © 2012 by Silver Strong & Associates. Adapted with permission.

Lesson or unit topic: _____

Questioning in Style Planning Form

MASTERY QUESTIONS
ask students to *remember facts and procedures:*

✓ Recall facts and formulas
✓ Observe and describe
✓ Locate, organize, or sequence
✓ Perform procedures/calculations with accuracy
✓ Define, restate, or summarize

My questions:

INTERPERSONAL QUESTIONS
ask students to *relate on a personal level:*

✓ Share their feelings, reactions, and opinions
✓ Draw connections to their own lives
✓ Assist or advise other people
✓ Put themselves in someone else's shoes
✓ Consider personal preferences and values

My questions:

UNDERSTANDING QUESTIONS
ask students to *reason, analyze, and explain:*

✓ Compare and contrast
✓ Explain, reason, or understand why or how
✓ Give reasons, evidence, and examples
✓ Analyze, interpret, evaluate, or conclude
✓ Classify or categorize

My questions:

SELF-EXPRESSIVE QUESTIONS
ask students to *create and explore possibilities:*

✓ Speculate (what if?), hypothesize, or predict
✓ Generate and explore alternatives
✓ Create or design something original
✓ Represent concepts visually/symbolically
✓ Develop and explore similes

My questions:

🌓 Teacher Talk

➔ Before using this tool for the first time, assess the "stylishness" of your *existing* questioning repertoire by recording how many of each style of question you ask during a given class period. Notice any patterns? If you favor certain styles over others, aim for a more balanced approach.

➔ Aim to incorporate all four styles of questions into written assignments and tests as well as classroom lectures and activities.

➔ Prepare students to be successful by modeling the kinds of thinking and responses that different question types require (e.g., show them how to respond successfully to a comparison question).

➔ The Questioning in Style framework can be used to develop a variety of critical thinking skills (e.g., retelling, comparing, supporting a position with evidence), to target all six categories in the cognitive domain of Bloom's Taxonomy, and to generate the kinds of "deep explanation questions" that studies show can improve academic performance (Pashler et al., 2007). Posing different styles of questions is also a great way to engage students with different interests and talents.

➔ Style-based questions can be used to do more than check for understanding while teaching. They can be used for a number of different purposes (e.g., to hook students' interest, help students access their prior knowledge, encourage reflection)—and at all stages of the instructional process. The ultimate goal is to pose different styles of questions throughout your lessons and units.

A Unit Blueprint Organizer like the one below (go to www.ThoughtfulClassroom.com/Tools to download a blank version) can help you achieve this goal.* Use the organizer to map out questions you can ask during each phase or "episode" of an upcoming lesson or unit. Then, pose these questions at the appropriate points in the lesson or unit. The questions that a math teacher developed for a unit on long division are shown here:

The Five Episodes of Effective Instruction	Questions I will ask during each episode	Style
1) *Preparing students for new learning* Establish purpose, spark interest, activate prior knowledge.	*How can you make a complex problem easier to solve?*	*Understanding*
2) *Presenting new learning* Present and help students engage with/acquire the content.	*Watch as I solve these two problems on the board. What are the steps in long division? Describe them.*	*Mastery*
3) *Deepening and reinforcing learning* Help students review, practice, and deepen their learning.	*What happens if you change or add a digit to the divisor or dividend? Experiment. Notice any patterns?*	*Self-Expressive*
4) *Applying learning* Challenge students to demonstrate and apply their learning.	*Two of the long-division problems on the board are incorrect. Can you locate and explain the errors?*	*Understanding*
5) *Reflecting on and celebrating learning* Help students reflect on and celebrate their learning.	*How did you feel about long division at the start of the unit? How do you feel now?*	*Interpersonal*

SOURCE: Adapted from *Tools for Thoughtful Assessment* (p. 71), by A. L. Boutz, H. F. Silver, J. W. Jackson, and M. J. Perini, 2012, Franklin Lakes, NJ: Thoughtful Education Press. © 2012 by Silver Strong & Associates. Adapted with permission.

*For more on the Thoughtful Classroom's Blueprint Model for lesson and unit design, see *Classroom Curriculum Design: How Strategic Units Improve Instruction and Engage Students in Meaningful Learning* (Silver & Perini, 2010a). For more on the Five Episodes of Effective Instruction, see the Appendix.

Variation: Assessment Tasks in Style

Developing different styles of assessment tasks is just as valuable as developing different styles of questions. Use the Task Creation Menu below to help you design different styles of tasks over the course of the year or to create "multi-style assignments" that contain all four styles of tasks in one (see the area and perimeter example at the bottom of the page).

TASK CREATION MENU	
To create a MASTERY TASK, you might ask students to • Recall important information—facts, formulas, dates, etc. • Define terms or concepts. • Demonstrate, describe, or follow a set of procedures. • Locate, match, or sequence information. • Make and label visual displays (e.g., charts, maps, diagrams). • Perform calculations or procedures with accuracy. • List or summarize information. • Describe details (who, what, when, where).	**To create an INTERPERSONAL TASK, you might ask students to** • Share feelings, reactions, or opinions about the content. • Connect or apply the content to their personal lives/experiences. • Teach, work with, or offer advice to other people. • Personify something. (If you were ___, what would you feel/do?) • Put themselves in someone else's shoes (real or fictional). • Use personal values to prioritize information or make decisions. • Communicate with others via letter, blog, diary entry, etc. • Role-play.
To create an UNDERSTANDING TASK, you might ask students to • Compare and contrast (facts, formulas, dates, characters, etc.). • Analyze causes and effects. • Support ideas with evidence and examples. • Explain why or how. • Classify, categorize, or make logical connections. • Generate and test hypotheses. • Make or evaluate decisions using specific criteria. • Analyze, interpret, or draw conclusions about data, texts, etc.	**To create a SELF-EXPRESSIVE TASK, you might ask students to** • Speculate or anticipate consequences. (What if ___?) • Represent concepts visually (e.g., using symbols, images, icons). • Create or invent something original (e.g., product, slogan, myth). • Visualize or free-associate. (What comes to mind when ___?) • Use similes to illustrate their understanding of key concepts. • Generate alternatives (e.g., solutions, endings, approaches). • Apply their learning to a new and different context. • Express their learning in a creative or artistic way.

SOURCE: Adapted from *Tools for Thoughtful Assessment* (p. 210), by A. L. Boutz, H. F. Silver, J. W. Jackson, and M. J. Perini, 2012, Franklin Lakes, NJ: Thoughtful Education Press. © 2012 by Silver Strong & Associates. Adapted with permission.

EXAMPLE: In honor of the fiftieth anniversary of the classic game Twister, a teacher developed the following collection of assessment tasks (one from each style) to check for understanding at the end of a unit on area and perimeter. Students demonstrated their skills by completing all four tasks.

MASTERY TASK	INTERPERSONAL TASK
A Twister game mat is rectangular, and it measures 67 inches by 55 inches. The diameter of each of the 24 colored circles is 7 inches. Calculate the area and perimeter of the board, the circumference of each circle, and the combined area of all the circles.	Think about what you've learned over the course of this unit. Write a letter to the students in next year's class that will help them understand what area and perimeter are, how to calculate them, and how area and perimeter are used in the real world.
UNDERSTANDING TASK	**SELF-EXPRESSIVE TASK**
Pretend you're deciding which of two games to play at a carnival. Both involve tossing a coin and having it land on a Twister mat. With Game A, you win when the coin lands on a colored circle. With Game B, you win when the coin lands on the white background. Which game do you have a better chance of winning? Explain why.	Create your own Twister-like game mat, but use colored triangles, rectangles, and squares instead of circles. Design your mat such that the area of the colored shapes is exactly half the area of the white background. Include a labeled sketch of your mat and show your work.

Scavenger Hunt

What is it?

A fun and engaging way to have students practice text-based search tasks (e.g., find a central idea, find a detail to support that idea, find evidence to support an author's claim)

What are the benefits of using this tool?

New standards and test items demand that we develop students' ability to search texts for specific details, evidence, and other kinds of information. On the other hand, an overreliance on reading worksheets to build this essential skill can lead to boredom, frustration, and disengagement. Enter Scavenger Hunt! This tool teaches students how to search texts actively, and it makes the search process engaging and enjoyable by using a scavenger hunt format. Introducing this tool early, and using it throughout the year, can help build one of the most important academic skills of all—and turn reading tasks into activities that students actually look forward to.

What are the basic steps?

1. Identify one or more reading standards that you've been working on with your students.

2. Design some "Find a ___" tasks that have ties to the selected standard(s). Tasks should be designed around one or more grade-appropriate texts/passages, and they should require searching those texts or passages for specific features, information, or evidence. See p. 77 for examples.

3. Record your tasks on the Scavenger Hunt form (p. 79), and distribute copies to students. Tell students whether to hunt for the items on their own or in teams and how to mark what they find (e.g., write on the text or use sticky notes). Emphasize that accuracy is more important than speed.

4. Give students copies of the text(s) they'll need to complete the assigned tasks, and instruct them to start hunting. If appropriate, number individual lines/paragraphs so students can more easily refer to what they've found. ("The words I chose are in lines two and three of paragraph four.")

5. Review and discuss students' responses as a class. ("Who wants to share what they found for this task?" "Can you explain why you selected this paragraph?" "Might this sentence be a better choice than that one? Why?" "Could both Sarah's and John's selections be correct? Why or why not?")

6. Encourage students to debate and defend conflicting responses (moderate as needed). Help them understand why one response is better than another or why multiple responses are equally valid.

Note: Teaching students to share, discuss, and defend their ideas in a respectful manner develops valuable speaking and listening skills.

7. Collect and review students' work to gain additional information about students' mastery of specific skills (e.g., which students are still having trouble finding details to support a main idea). Work with students individually or as a class to develop any skills they haven't yet mastered.

How is this tool used in the classroom?

✔ To develop students' ability to find textual features, information, and evidence

✔ To turn text-based search tasks into tasks that students enjoy

✔ To assess and improve students' ability to handle text-based test questions

Find-it tasks can be designed around a variety of reading standards and skills. For example:

If your standards ask students to do this…	Your find-it tasks might look like this…
Search for factual information and explanations that are explicitly stated within the text.	• How did Pascal keep his red balloon dry? FIND a picture that tells us. • Why is the USS *Constitution* called "Old Ironsides"? FIND the explanation. • FIND two human behaviors/activities that contribute to global warming.
Find textual evidence to support inferences and conclusions.	• FIND two words or pictures that might lead us to infer that the bear is angry. • FIND two sentences from the passage that support the following conclusion… • FIND one detail from each source that supports the answer to Part A.
Identify central ideas and themes, and summarize supporting details and ideas.	• FIND the paragraph that best reflects the main idea of the passage as a whole. • Read the main idea below. FIND two details from the text that support this idea.
Find details that reveal important information about (or highlight relationships between) characters, settings, events, and individuals.	• How can we tell that the narrator is a generous individual? FIND some evidence. • FIND two details from the story that help create the setting. • FIND lines in the poem that reveal the effect the incident had on the narrator. • How did Franklin's work influence Watson and Crick? FIND some evidence.
Find clues to the meaning of words and phrases as they're used in a text or words that affect tone or meaning.	• FIND a phrase that helps us grasp the meaning of *savage* as it's used here. • FIND words that contribute to the informal tone of this letter.
Find connections between individual structural elements (e.g., sentences, paragraphs, scenes, chapters), and recognize how individual elements contribute to the development of ideas and/or fit into the overall text structure.	• In this passage, the author discusses two seemingly unrelated concepts. How does he connect them? FIND a sentence that makes this connection. • Examine the colonists' argument for independence. FIND the section(s) whose purpose is to demonstrate that the colonists had tried to work things out with the king.
Find passages that reveal or reflect an author's point of view or purpose, as well as passages that distinguish (or highlight similarities) between two separate points of view.	• FIND a sentence that clarifies the author's position on this issue. • How does the author address conflicting viewpoints? FIND some examples. • How can we tell the author believes the theft was justified? FIND evidence.
Interpret information that's presented in diverse formats, including visually and quantitatively.	• FIND a picture that shows the Very Hungry Caterpillar isn't feeling well. • FIND the portion of this chart that supports the author's claim. • Can you FIND any evidence for a regional trend in flu cases? Look in all three of the provided sources: the map, the data table, and the CDC bulletin.
Identify the components, strengths, and weaknesses of an argument.	• FIND two specific reasons that support the author's claim. • FIND a piece of evidence that isn't relevant to the author's argument.
Compare two or more texts, and identify similarities and differences in content, focus, style, etc.	• Read these creation myths. FIND some common elements. • FIND information in Source 1 that conflicts with Source 2. • FIND rhetorical features that are common to both texts.

SOURCE: Adapted from *Tools for Conquering the Common Core* (p. 42), by H. F. Silver and A. L. Boutz, 2015, Franklin Lakes, NJ: Thoughtful Education Press. © 2015 by Silver Strong & Associates. Adapted with permission.

⬤ Teacher Talk

➜ To simplify things for primary-grade students, English language learners, students with reading disabilities, or students who are new to the tool, you can use shorter, less complex text passages (read them aloud if needed), design multiple-choice tasks rather than open-ended ones (e.g., "Which two of the statements below support the author's claim?"), or have students hunt for items as a class or in groups rather than on their own.

➜ This tool can be used at multiple points in an instructional sequence. Use it for diagnostic purposes at the start of a unit or school year. (What do students know already?) Use it for formative assessment purposes in the middle of a unit or school year. (Which skills still need work?) Use it summatively to determine which skills students have mastered by the end of a unit or school year.

➜ When creating your tasks, think carefully about how long it will take students to read the required passages—particularly if you're working with beginning readers or students with learning disabilities. Be careful not to create more tasks than students can complete in the allotted time.

➜ Move beyond traditional printed texts; have students "hunt" through videos, audio clips, charts, etc.

➜ Since friendly competition can increase student engagement, some teachers turn Scavenger Hunt into a game in which students compete for points (one point for each correct item; the student/team that's first to find all items correctly gets three bonus points, second-to-finish gets two, etc.). Besides being fun for students, low-stakes games that target essential content have been linked to significant gains in learning and achievement (Haystead & Marzano, 2009).

➜ If students will hunt in teams rather than on their own, set things up so all team members have a role to play. At the minimum, everyone should have to discuss and agree on the final responses.

➜ You can use find-it tasks as starting points from which to initiate more in-depth analyses of the targeted textual elements. You might, for example, start by challenging students to find aspects of a live production that depart from the original script—and then pose follow-up questions whose purpose is to help students analyze the purpose and impact of the changes they identified. ("Why might the director have chosen to make these changes? What impact did they have? Do you feel the changes were good ones? Why or why not?")

➜ As written, the tool focuses on find-it tasks that have ties to *reading* skills and standards, but you can design find-it tasks around other ELA skills and standards as well. To target language skills rather than reading skills, for example, you might give students a piece of writing and ask them to find grammar errors, spelling errors, or words and phrases whose level of formality doesn't match the rest of the piece.

Scavenger Hunt

Text(s) to search:

My task:

Here's where I found what I was looking for (include page, paragraph, or line number if appropriate):

Text(s) to search:

My task:

Here's where I found what I was looking for (include page, paragraph, or line number if appropriate):

Text(s) to search:

My task:

Here's where I found what I was looking for (include page, paragraph, or line number if appropriate):

4

Developing a Culture
of Thinking and Learning

**How can I develop a classroom culture that promotes
serious learning and sophisticated forms of thinking?**

Learning without thought is labor lost; thought without learning is perilous.

—Confucius

*Much like the home, school provides the comfort and care of a safe environment
for thinking. It affords thoughtful lessons as catalysts for growth and development.
School provides the time for learning through the toil of trial and error. And, in
the end, school as a home for the mind fosters the reflective moments that anchor
learning for a lifetime.*

—Robin Fogarty, from the Foreword to *The School as a Home for the Mind:
Creating Mindful Curriculum, Instruction, and Dialogue, 2nd Edition*

Charlotte Danielson (2007), one of the foremost experts on teacher effectiveness, tells
us that the most effective teachers strive to build "classrooms with a strong culture
for learning" (p. 67). As its name suggests, our fourth cornerstone draws on the work
that Danielson has done to define what a culture of learning looks like. However, the
Confucius quotation at the head of this chapter reminds us that thinking and learning
go hand in hand. Thus, we have given *thinking* an equal emphasis in this cornerstone
called A Culture of Thinking and Learning.

This fourth and final cornerstone is dedicated to the promise that we make to all our
students: school is a place where we take thinking and learning seriously. Therefore,
in our classrooms, ideas will be valued and students will learn to use their minds well.

But what does this mean? It means that in order to be effective educators, we must
help our students acquire the kinds of sophisticated thinking skills that promote deep
learning and facilitate academic success—skills like understanding and using critical
vocabulary, supporting claims with evidence, and debating ideas respectfully.

In this chapter, we present five tools that you can use to develop students' critical thinking capacities and increase students' power as learners:

1. **3C Word Walls** transforms classroom word walls from passive displays to interactive learning tools that promote three critical Cs: **C**omprehension, **C**ommunication skills, and **C**ollege and career readiness.

2. **Because** trains students to support their ideas with evidence by asking them to give a "because" for every statement they make and answer they give.

3. **Forced Choice** sparks discussion and debate around critical topics by inviting students to develop and defend positions on content-related controversies.

4. **The Power of Pause** shows students how a strategy as simple as pausing to think has the power to promote metacognition, deepen comprehension, and improve learning.

5. **Power Previewing** prepares students to get more out of assigned texts by familiarizing them with previewing strategies that expert readers use to help them understand, actively engage with, and enjoy what they read.

3C Word Walls

What is it?

A tool that helps students learn—and learn to use—critical academic vocabulary by transforming classroom word walls from passive displays to interactive learning tools

What are the benefits of using this tool?

Many tools claim to build students' vocabularies. But are they effective? Effective vocabulary instruction requires students to think deeply about and actually *learn* new words, not memorize definitions. And it focuses on useful words, not trivial ones—the kinds of words that can enhance **C**omprehension, **C**ommunication skills, and **C**ollege and career readiness (the 3Cs in the tool's title). This tool explains how to develop these three critical Cs using four different types of word walls: domain-specific word walls, descriptive word walls, transitional word walls, and "task and test verb" word walls. By outlining concrete suggestions for getting students to engage with and use word-wall terms, it promotes deeper word knowledge than many traditional vocabulary tools.

What are the basic steps?

1. Familiarize yourself with the different types of word walls described on pp. 84–87.* Decide which type you'll create and the words that you'll include.

2. Record your words on index cards or strips of paper. (Words should be large enough for students to see from their seats.) Ensure that students will be able to rearrange and interact with the words by hanging them on an easily accessible board using tacks, magnets, or Velcro.

3. Introduce the word wall. (What type is it? What kind of words are on it? What is its purpose?)

4. Teach or review the meanings of the words using any strategies you want. (You can do this all at once or over the course of a unit.) Post a student-friendly definition for each word.

Tip: Invite students to personalize and take ownership of the wall by adding images, drawings, synonyms/antonyms, examples, and/or objects that help them grasp the meanings of the words.

5. Use word-wall terms as often as possible when speaking and writing (point to the wall or underline the words to help students make the connection). Encourage students to do the same.

6. Make word-wall activities part of your regular classroom routine. Ideas for getting students to engage with, use, and demonstrate their knowledge of word-wall terms can be found on pp. 84–87.

7. Facilitate continued use of word-wall terms by making them accessible throughout the year. When a new wall goes up, store old words in a recipe-card box, on a key ring, etc.

How is this tool used in the classroom?

✔ To help students develop a rich and varied vocabulary of domain-specific and general terms

✔ To promote comprehension, communication skills, and college and career readiness

*The standards referenced on pp. 84–87 are from the Common Core ELA/Literacy Standards (NGA Center/CCSSO, 2010a) and the Next Generation Science Standards (NGSS Lead States, 2013).

Domain-Specific Word Walls

Description/Purpose:

Domain-specific word walls develop students' understanding of discipline-specific terms and concepts from particular units of study.

How these word walls develop the 3Cs:

These walls promote **C**ollege and career readiness by helping students learn a wide range of discipline-specific vocabulary terms. Possessing this type of vocabulary knowledge enables students to better **C**omprehend critical course material and to **C**ommunicate more precisely, using the language of experts in the field.

Creating your wall:

Select discipline-specific terms that relate to one or more units of study (e.g., the boldface words from a textbook chapter). Keep things manageable by limiting the terms you select to ones that are critical to understanding the content. Note that terms can be anything from people to places to symbols, abbreviations, or dates.

Example: A high school English teacher selected the following terms for a segment on sonnets: *sonnet, rhyme scheme, iambic pentameter, quatrain, couplet, Shakespeare,* and *Petrarch.*

Example: A US government teacher selected the following terms as part of a unit on the lawmaking process: *legislate, lobby, enact, vote, campaign, debate, override, compromise, filibuster,* and *amend.*

Ideas for getting students to engage with, use, and demonstrate their knowledge of word-wall terms:

- Play "use it or lose it" (students can play on their own or as part of a team). Award points for using word-wall terms in conversations, in written assignments, and/or on tests. The student (or team) with the most points at the end of a specified time period wins.

- Play "missed opportunity." Give students buzzers. Encourage them to buzz any time there's a missed word-wall opportunity (a place where you or a classmate could've used a word-wall term to express an idea more precisely but didn't). Have them explain what the term is and how it could have been used to express the original speaker's idea more precisely.

- Invite students to define word-wall terms using the method(s) of their choice. Possibilities include crafting original and student-friendly definitions, listing critical attributes, developing similes or sketches that capture meaning, or making/explaining connections to other words on the wall.

- Require students to use a specific number of word-wall terms when completing a written assignment or test question. ("In order to get full credit, you must include three word-wall terms.")

- Challenge students to incorporate as many terms as possible into a story, summary, or other piece of writing.

- Develop and test big-picture understanding by challenging students to identify and explain connections between two or more terms on the wall (e.g., "a *pulley* is a type of *simple machine,*" "a *chick* is a baby *bird,*" or "*weight-bearing activities* like *jogging* and *dancing* develop *bone strength*").

- When appropriate, encourage students to explore the ways that word-wall terms are used outside your particular discipline (e.g., a "magnetic personality" versus "magnetic" in a science context).

- Invite students to illustrate the meanings of word-wall terms. Post the sketches that best capture the terms' meanings on the word wall. (Note that teaching students to clarify ideas/information using visuals is considered a valuable college and career readiness skill; see, for example, Common Core ELA/Literacy Standard SL.CCR.5.)

SOURCE: Adapted from *Tools for Conquering the Common Core* (p. 112), by H. F. Silver and A. L. Boutz, 2015, Franklin Lakes, NJ: Thoughtful Education Press. © 2015 by Silver Strong & Associates. Adapted with permission.

Descriptive Word Walls

Description/Purpose:

Descriptive word walls expose students to the kinds of "awesome adjectives" and "va-va-voom verbs" that experts use to make their writing vivid, specific, and interesting.

How these word walls develop the 3Cs:

These word walls help students develop the kind of rich and varied vocabulary that today's **C**ollege and career readiness standards call for. As such, they empower students both to **C**omprehend complex texts and to **C**ommunicate in ways that meet the standards' demands for precise language and descriptive details (see, for example, specific grade-level expectations within Common Core ELA/Literacy Standards W.CCR.2–3, SL.CCR.4, and L.CCR.3).

Creating your wall:

Whenever possible, select verbs and adjectives (add adverbs if you want) that you can connect to a topic, theme, or text you're covering in class. Choosing words that are linked to your content in some way will make the words easier for you and your students to use in classroom conversations and writing assignments. It also gives the words context, which can make them more meaningful and memorable for students.

Example: A primary-grade teacher used a Halloween-themed unit to introduce this group of interesting verbs and adjectives: *spook, howl, screech, petrified, eerie.*

Example: A social studies teacher created a descriptive word wall around her Age of Exploration unit by selecting verbs and adjectives that describe the explorers (*resolute, daring, bold, weather-beaten*), the things they did (*embark, navigate, persist, subjugate*), and their journeys (*arduous, interminable, treacherous, fortuitous*).

Example: A math teacher prepared students to describe data trends on charts and graphs more precisely by posting these words on her wall: *rise, drop, climb, plateau, gradual, steady, steep, sharp, dramatic, mild.*

Note: While the words on this kind of wall can have connections to the content that students are studying, they shouldn't be *specific* to that content or content area. Instead, they should be general terms that students would likely encounter in a wide range of texts and contexts (i.e., the "general academic" or "Tier Two" terms referred to in both Language Standard 6 and Appendix A from the Common Core ELA/Literacy Standards [NGA Center/CCSSO, 2010a]).

Ideas for getting students to engage with, use, and demonstrate their knowledge of word-wall terms:

- Challenge students to make an existing piece of writing (theirs, yours, or a published sample) more interesting and/or precise by replacing some of the existing words with word-wall terms.

- Encourage students to expand their vocabularies by finding and posting synonyms for word-wall terms.

- Address college and career readiness standards that focus on nuances in word meaning (e.g., Common Core ELA/Literacy Standard L.CCR.5) by helping students explore subtle differences between related words. In the Halloween-themed wall described above, for example, you might discuss the similarities and differences between *shrieking* and *howling* (both involve loud sounds, but not equivalent ones).

- Address college and career readiness standards that focus on word relationships (e.g., Common Core ELA/Literacy Standard L.CCR.5) by asking students to show their grasp of word-wall terms by relating them to their opposites (antonyms) and to words with similar but not identical meanings (synonyms).

- Challenge students to include a specific number of word-wall terms in a description, summary, explanation, or narrative. Have them underline the terms for easy finding/counting.

- Create a fill-in-the-blank piece that students can complete using word-wall terms. Discuss it as a class.

- Have students find real-world or literary examples of the terms (e.g., animals that are *furry*, stories that are *inspiring*, characters who are *courageous*, or athletes who *persevere* through challenges).

SOURCE: Adapted from *Tools for Conquering the Common Core* (p. 114), by H. F. Silver and A. L. Boutz, 2015, Franklin Lakes, NJ: Thoughtful Education Press. © 2015 by Silver Strong & Associates. Adapted with permission.

Transitional Word Walls

Description/Purpose:

Transitional word walls familiarize students with linking and organizing words like *first*, *after that*, *in contrast*, and *as a result*.

How these word walls develop the 3Cs:

Making students aware of transitional words and their functions prepares them to better **C**omprehend the structure and meaning of assigned texts. Encouraging students to use these words when speaking and writing helps them **C**ommunicate in the kind of clear and coherent way that today's **C**ollege and career readiness standards demand (see, for example, Common Core ELA/Literacy Standards W.CCR.1–4 and SL.CCR.4).

Creating your wall:

Select transitional words that are both age appropriate and consistent with the type(s) of writing tasks you'll be focusing on in class. The list of linking and organizing words on p. 88 presents a variety of options to choose from.

Example: *First*, *next*, *then*, *after that*, and *finally* would be good choices for writing tasks that involve describing a series of steps or events.

Example: *On the contrary*, *on the other hand*, *conversely*, and *alternatively* would be good choices for writing tasks that involve presenting contrasting viewpoints.

Ideas for getting students to engage with, use, and demonstrate their knowledge of word-wall terms:

- Write (or have students write) a piece that includes at least five word-wall terms. Erase the word-wall terms, replace them with blank lines, and challenge students to fill in the blanks with appropriate terms. Review students' choices as a class. Highlight the idea that different words can be correct (e.g., you could introduce the second event in a sequence with *second*, *next*, *then*, or *after that*).

- Challenge students to include word-wall terms in an explanation, summary, argument/opinion piece, lab report, or narrative. Have them underline the terms for easy finding.

  Example (explanation): _First, I subtracted two from both sides of the equation. Then_ . . .

  Example (argument piece): _Whereas some might argue that this kind of art has no place in_ . . .

  Example (lab report): _For this reason, we decided to check the pH of our solution. Since it was low_ . . .

  Example (narrative): _All in all, it was a great experience._

- Give students samples of a specific type of writing piece (e.g., sequence, cause/effect, comparison). Have them underline the linking words and discuss the role that these words play in the overall structure and organization of this type of piece. Were the linking words used to connect a series of events? (*first, next, after that*) Present an outcome? (*as a result, consequently, thus*) Highlight similarities? (*similarly, in the same way, likewise*)

- Help students explore different kinds of linking words by having them organize a collection of these words into functional categories and give each category a descriptive label (e.g., *comparison words, order words, clarification words*). See p. 88 for some sample groupings.

SOURCE: Adapted from *Tools for Conquering the Common Core* (p. 113), by H. F. Silver and A. L. Boutz, 2015, Franklin Lakes, NJ: Thoughtful Education Press. © 2015 by Silver Strong & Associates. Adapted with permission.

"Task and Test Verb" Word Walls

Description/Purpose:

"Task and test verb" word walls feature the types of thinking and test-taking verbs that appear in task descriptions, test questions, and college and career readiness standards—verbs like *compare*, *calculate*, *explain*, and *analyze*.

How these word walls develop the 3Cs:

These word walls familiarize students with verbs they're likely to encounter on test questions and tasks, particularly questions and tasks that are aligned with **C**ollege and career readiness standards. Understanding these verbs prepares students to **C**omprehend these types of questions/tasks more easily and **C**ommunicate appropriate responses (i.e., responses that both address the question and reflect their understanding of the relevant material).

Creating your wall:

Select verbs that reflect the demands of standards documents and standards-based assessment tests. (A list of possibilities is provided on p. 89.) You can select your verbs at random, go in order from most to least used (which verbs appear most frequently in the standards for your particular grade level?), or choose verbs that reflect the thinking demands, assessment tasks, and test questions associated with an upcoming instructional unit. Regardless of how you choose your verbs, be selective. Focus on a few at a time so that students can learn them deeply.

Example: If lesson plans call for students to *observe* plants and animals so as to *compare* the diversity of life in different habitats (Next Generation Science Standard 2-LS4-1), you might put the terms *observe* and *compare* on your word wall.

Example: Prepare students for computerized assessment tests by familiarizing them with words such as *scroll*, *click*, *drag and drop*, and *highlight*.

Note: Remember to teach thinking and test-taking verbs in the same way you'd teach "regular" vocabulary terms—by defining, modeling, giving examples, and checking for understanding.

Ideas for getting students to engage with, use, and demonstrate their knowledge of word-wall terms:

* Encourage students to define the terms using language that makes sense to them. For example, "If I am asked to *retell* something, it means I should tell it again in my own words."

* Have students compare and contrast potentially confusing terms (e.g., "What's the difference between *persuading* and *arguing*?" or "What's the difference between *estimating* and *calculating*?").

* Generate questions/tasks that include word-wall terms in the instructions (e.g., "*Compare* the two accounts of this event"). Use students' responses to evaluate their understanding of the terms in question (e.g., did they actually *compare* the two accounts when writing their responses?). Redefine and review any terms that students are unclear about.

* Invite students to generate study questions that include word-wall terms. Have them respond to their own questions, exchange questions with a partner, or submit their questions to you for possible inclusion on a future test.

* Invite students to "play teacher." Find (or generate) an incorrect response to a short-answer question that can be traced to a misunderstood verb. Have students identify and explain where the test-taker went wrong. ("The question asked you to *compare* velocity and acceleration, but all you did was *describe* them. To *compare*, you would've had to explain how they were similar and different.")

SOURCE: Adapted from *Tools for Conquering the Common Core* (p. 115), by H. F. Silver and A. L. Boutz, 2015, Franklin Lakes, NJ: Thoughtful Education Press. © 2015 by Silver Strong & Associates. Adapted with permission.

Linking and Organizing Words

To show order or time

First	Second	Next	Then	After that	Finally
Before	At the same time	Subsequently	In the meantime	While	The next step
Earlier	Lastly	First of all	In the first place	To begin with	In conclusion

To introduce facts, reasons, evidence, examples, or additional points

For example	One reason	Another reason	One example	Another example	For instance
First of all	Second of all	Additionally	And	Also	Finally
In addition	Furthermore	Moreover	What's more	As it says here …	As __ notes, "__."

To draw comparisons

Similarly	In the same way	By the same token	Correspondingly	In comparison	Likewise
One similarity	Another similarity	Both	All	As a group	Collectively

To highlight differences or present contrasting ideas/viewpoints

One difference	Another difference	Actually	In fact	On the contrary	In reality
In contrast	However	Although	Instead	But	Yet
Rather	Alternatively	Conversely	On the other hand	Another possibility	Whereas

To conclude, summarize, or discuss causes/effects

To summarize	In conclusion	Finally	As a result	Therefore	Thus
All in all	As expected	On the whole	For these reasons	As shown here	Consequently
Taken together	Because	So	If … then …	Since	In that case

To generalize

In general	On the whole	As a rule	Typically	In most cases	For the most part

To emphasize

Note that	Remember that	Above all	Especially	Importantly	What's more

To clarify

For example	For instance	In other words	To clarify	Specifically	Put another way

SOURCE: From *Tools for Conquering the Common Core* (p. 77), by H. F. Silver and A. L. Boutz, 2015, Franklin Lakes, NJ: Thoughtful Education Press. © 2015 by Silver Strong & Associates. Reprinted with permission.

Task and Test Verbs

Acknowledge	**Develop**	Organize
Add to	Distinguish	Paraphrase
Address	**Drag / Drag and drop**	Predict
Analyze	**Draw / Draw on**	Prove
Apply	Edit	Provide
Articulate	**Elaborate**	Quote
Assess	Eliminate	Recount
Build / Build on	Emphasize	**Refer to / Reference**
Calculate	Estimate	Relate
Cite	**Evaluate**	Represent
Clarify	**Explain**	Retell
Classify	Express	Reveal
Click	Generate	Review
Compare	Graph	Revise
Complete	Highlight	Round
Conclude	Identify	Select
Consult	Illustrate	Solve
Contrast	Imply	Specify
Contribute to	Infer	**State/Restate**
Critique	Influence	Suggest
Defend	**Integrate**	**Summarize**
Define	**Interpret**	Supply
Delineate	Introduce	**Support**
Demonstrate	**Justify**	**Synthesize**
Describe	Locate	Trace
Determine	Measure	Verify

Note: This list was generated following an analysis of the Common Core State Standards, the Next Generation Science Standards, and sample test items from the Partnership for Assessment of Readiness for College and Careers (PARCC) and the Smarter Balanced Assessment Consortium. The twenty verbs that we believe are most critical to know appear in bold.

SOURCE: Adapted from *Tools for Conquering the Common Core* (p. 122), by H. F. Silver and A. L. Boutz, 2015, Franklin Lakes, NJ: Thoughtful Education Press. © 2015 by Silver Strong & Associates. Adapted with permission.

Because

What is it?

A tool that teaches students to support their thinking with reasons and evidence by encouraging them to provide a "because" for every claim they make or answer they give ("Curious George is a good name for this character *because* ..." "That strategy won't work *because* ...")

What are the benefits of using this tool?

Some habits of mind are so integral to good thinking that we want to instill them in our students starting on the very first day of school. One such habit is the "evidence habit"—or the understanding that ideas, opinions, and claims should always be backed by reasons and evidence. The Because tool offers a simple way to build and reinforce this evidence habit.[*] Regular use of the tool helps build a culture in which student behaviors such as elaborating on ideas, justifying conclusions, and testing one's own thinking become part of the everyday classroom experience.

What are the basic steps?

1. Tell students that you want them to start giving you a *because* for every answer they give and claim they make. ("I think Jimi Hendrix is the greatest guitar player of all time *because* ...")

2. Remind students to do this by writing the word *because* in an easily visible location (e.g., on the board or on a piece of poster paper). If students forget to give you a "because," prompt them to do so by pointing at the word. For example:

    Teacher: Is the solution on the board correct?

    Student: No. [Teacher points at the word *because* to remind the student to continue talking.]

    Student: Because you forgot to follow the order of operations.

3. Use students' responses to gauge their understanding of the material and their ability to support a claim with evidence, reasons, and examples. Respond accordingly.

---

[*]The Because technique was initially developed by Cathy Mitchell, a teacher at Robert Kerr Elementary School in Durand, MI. The figures in Examples 2–6 are reprinted with permission from a previously published version of this tool (Boutz et al., 2012, pp. 63–64).

How is this tool used in the classroom?

✔ To get students in the habit of supporting their ideas with reasons, evidence, and examples

✔ To check for depth of understanding

Besides getting students in the habit of supporting their responses with evidence, this tool can be used to test students' command of specific content knowledge, skills, and standards—and to help students reflect on their thinking and reasoning processes (Why do I think what I think? How do I know what I know?). The examples that follow illustrate these different uses.

Note: Although the Because technique was initially designed to be used during classroom lectures and discussions, you can use it with written assignments as well; see Examples 1, 4, and 5 for ideas.

EXAMPLE 1: Ask students to identify and explain flaws in logic or procedures

A high school math teacher posts an incorrectly solved problem on the board at the start of every class period and challenges his students to explain what's wrong. ("This solution is incorrect *because* …") Assigning this type of task gives him immediate feedback about students' grasp of the relevant content. It also develops his students' ability to identify and explain flaws in logic and reasoning—a key goal of the math standards that his state has adopted.

EXAMPLE 2: Ask students to share and justify their opinions during a discussion

A first-grade teacher uses this tool to have students share and justify their opinions about books they've read. Sometimes she has students share their opinions during classroom discussions (see sample dialogue below); other times, she targets argument-writing skills and standards by having students present and support their opinions in writing.

Teacher:	What did you think of *Alexander and the Terrible, Horrible, No Good, Very Bad Day*?
Student:	I liked it.
Teacher:	*Because?*
Student:	*Because* it reminded me of me.
Teacher:	*Because?*
Student:	*Because* I once had a bad day like that.
Teacher:	Anything else?
Student:	I also liked the book *because* the pictures were funny.

EXAMPLE 3: Check for understanding during a lecture

A high school biology teacher develops and tests critical content knowledge by posing "take-a-position questions" that require students to support their responses with relevant facts and details.

Teacher:	Does everyone agree with John that DNA and RNA are more similar than different?
Student 1:	I agree *because* they both have sugar-phosphate backbones. And *because* they both carry genetic information.
Student 2:	Another reason to agree is *because* three of the four nitrogenous bases in DNA and RNA are the same.
Student 3:	I disagree *because* they have different sugars (deoxyribose versus ribose), bases (uracil versus thymine), and functions.

EXAMPLE 4: Check for understanding at the end of an instructional episode

A second-grade teacher designed the worksheet below to test her students' understanding of critical shape attributes.

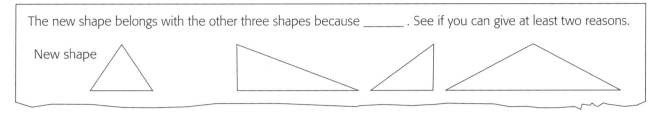

The new shape belongs with the other three shapes because _____ . See if you can give at least two reasons.

New shape

EXAMPLE 5: Check for understanding on a test

A computer science teacher often includes "because" questions on his end-of-unit tests. One of these questions and a student's response is shown here:

Question 6: Why might someone argue that Linux is better than the more commonly used operating systems that we've discussed? Give at least four reasons.

Because Linux is free to obtain.

Because Linux has fewer security issues (viruses, spyware, adware).

Because open-source software is a major advantage. You can use and modify the source code.

Because there's a large community of users constantly adding and improving programs.

EXAMPLE 6: Test students' reading comprehension

A team of elementary teachers uses the Because tool to test students' understanding of literary and informational texts. After reading (or having students read) a designated text, these teachers pose different kinds of checking-for-understanding questions and have students support their responses with specific examples from the text. They vary the kinds of questions they ask to test different dimensions of comprehension and address different Common Core Reading Standards (see below for two examples; the specific standards being addressed in each case are noted in parentheses).

Teacher: We just read two fables from different cultures. How are these fables similar? (Common Core RL.2.9)

Student 1: They are similar *because* they both have animals as their main characters.

Student 2: They are similar *because* the animal you don't expect to win ends up winning.

Student 3: They are similar *because* they teach you the same lesson.

Teacher: Does the author of this article present a convincing argument that coral reefs are in trouble? (Common Core RI.4.7, RI.4.8)

Student 1: Yes, *because* the graph shows that reefs are disappearing at an alarming rate—twice as fast as rainforests!

Student 2: Yes, *because* the article shows pictures of what the reefs look like now versus what they looked like before.

EXAMPLE 7: Encourage students to analyze their thinking and reasoning processes

A middle school social studies teacher regularly asks students to explain how they know what they know and why they think what they think. Getting students to talk through their responses in this way enables them (and her) to evaluate the quality of their thinking and reasoning processes.

Teacher:	How did you come to the conclusion that the Stamp Act helped lead to the American Revolution?
Student:	*Because* the Stamp Act really angered a lot of colonists.
Teacher:	*Because?*
Student:	*Because* the Stamp Act was a tax, and they didn't think it was a fair one.
Teacher:	*Because?*
Student:	*Because* they felt it was unfair to be taxed without representation in Parliament.
Teacher:	True, but is it really fair to say that the Stamp Act actually contributed to the revolution?
Student:	Yes, *because* the taxation issue it raised didn't go away. With each new unfair tax, more colonists wanted to rebel.

🌐 Teacher Talk

➔ Students are more likely to use *becauses* in their speaking and writing if they understand why those *becauses* are valuable. An easy way to help students see the difference a simple *because* can make is to present them with pairs of statements like the ones below, ask them to decide which statement in each pair is more powerful, and have them explain why. ("I think the *b* statements are more powerful because they give you more information" or "I think the *b* statements are better because they give you reasons. They don't just give you a *what*, they give you a *why*.")

> a) The corn plants didn't grow.
> b) The corn plants didn't grow because they didn't have enough water or sunlight to survive.
>
> a) I liked the book.
> b) I liked the book because it was about football, my favorite sport.
>
> a) The reading assignment was difficult.
> b) The reading assignment was difficult because it had a lot of vocabulary words I didn't know.

➔ If you consistently prompt students to include *because* in their responses, they'll get to the point where they feel a response is missing something if it doesn't include a *because*. When visiting classrooms that use this tool on a regular basis, we've actually seen students ask each other for a *because*. ("Hey, where's your *because*?")

➔ This tool gets students in the habit of supporting their ideas with reasons and evidence—a goal of many standards documents, including the Common Core ELA/Literacy Standards (NGA Center/CCSSO, 2010a), the Common Core Mathematics Standards (NGA Center/CCSSO, 2010b), and the Next Generation Science Standards (NGSS Lead States, 2013).

Forced Choice

What is it?

A tool that engages students in discussing and reviewing critical content (also practicing their argument skills) by requiring them to take and defend positions on content-related "controversies"

What are the benefits of using this tool?

Have you ever heard students having thoughtful and spirited conversations about chemical reactions, the Enlightenment, or the metric system? Forced Choice uses controversy, a known motivator and achievement booster (Lowry & Johnson, 1981), to get students engaged in discussing and debating critical content—even content they don't typically get excited about. At the heart of the tool are simple frames that force students to take and defend a position on a given topic or issue. The debates that these frames spark tend to be animated and enthusiastic ones, as most students relish the opportunity to express and make a case for their ideas. But the tool does more than promote engagement. By encouraging students to develop, discuss, and defend their ideas, Forced Choice requires them to think deeply about the relevant content and hone critical discussion skills, including listening carefully, disagreeing respectfully, and supporting ideas with evidence.

What are the basic steps?

1. Review the Forced Choice frames on pp. 96–97. Pick one that appeals to you and fits your content.

2. Use the selected frame to develop a content-specific question or statement that will provoke debate when presented to students. Confirm that your question or statement is one that students can have legitimately different opinions about, not one that has a definitive right or wrong answer.

   Note: The goal is to develop questions or statements that require students to explore and think deeply about the relevant content (review important details, clarify key concepts, etc.).

3. Present your question or statement. Give students time to develop a position and gather evidence. Clarify that there are no right or wrong answers, just different opinions.

4. Prepare students to engage in a heated but respectful discussion by reviewing and modeling the following discussion guidelines (modify the list as needed):

   • State your positions clearly. Support them with relevant facts, reasons, and evidence.

   • Treat your classmates as you'd want to be treated. If you're going to disagree, do it respectfully.

   • Question and critique each other's logic and evidence, not each other's intelligence.

   • Be passionate about your positions, but listen to other people's arguments as well.

   • Keep an open mind. Feel free to change positions in response to what you hear.

5. Invite students to share and justify their positions. Moderate the discussion by helping students recognize faulty or insufficient evidence, transform personal attacks into thoughtful critiques, etc.

6. Help students reflect on what they learned and how well they followed the discussion guidelines.

How is this tool used in the classroom?

✔ To promote active conversations about (and a deeper understanding of) critical content

✔ To use controversy and debate as a means of stimulating student engagement

✔ To develop students' ability to support a position with solid reasons and evidence

✔ To develop essential speaking and listening skills

Teachers use the Forced Choice frames described on pp. 96–97 to engage students in discussing key content and discussing it excitedly. Sample prompts show how the frames can work across grade levels and content areas.

🌐 Teacher Talk

→ Remind students to support their "forced choices" with reasons and evidence by saying, "And you chose that position *because*?" (Students should respond with, "I think ___ because ___.") For a more detailed look at this approach, see the Because tool (pp. 90–93).

→ Forced Choice provides an ideal opportunity to review and give students feedback about their use of behavioral guidelines that relate to sharing and discussing ideas—guidelines like listening carefully, disagreeing respectfully, and critiquing ideas rather than people. As always, remember to teach expected behaviors explicitly, provide reminders as needed, and offer specific and informative praise to students who exhibit the behaviors successfully. ("I appreciate that you questioned Santiago's logic rather than attacking Santiago personally.")

→ Despite its seemingly contentious nature, Forced Choice is actually an ideal tool for teaching students how to compromise. Once students have laid out their arguments, consider asking them whether compromise is possible. ("Can you come up with a position statement that everyone in the class can agree with?") Students who are arguing about the merits of genetically modified foods, for example, might agree to the following compromise: "Genetically modified foods should at least be labeled so consumers can avoid them if they want to."

→ Be sure to leave time for reflection (Step 6). Help students solidify their understanding of the relevant content (and demonstrate they were listening) by challenging them to summarize their classmates' positions and evidence. Prepare students to become more actively and appropriately engaged in future discussions by helping them assess—and think about how to improve—their performance. ("How well did you personally follow our discussion guidelines? How well did the class as a whole follow the guidelines? How can you/we do better next time?")

→ This tool supports the Common Core ELA/Literacy Standards (NGA Center/CCSSO, 2010a) and other ELA/literacy standards' call to engage students in structured conversations around critical content and develop students' argument skills, particularly the ability to support a position with evidence. As written, the tool develops oral argument skills, but you can target written argument skills instead by having students present and justify their positions in writing rather than orally.

Six Forced Choice Frames

More Alike or Different?

More Alike or Different? is useful when students are studying related pairs of items, events, concepts, or individuals. To use this frame, have students review what they know about each item, decide whether the items are more alike or different, and support their choices with relevant details. Asking students to decide whether two items are more alike or different and explain their reasoning forces them to examine the items more closely and attend to the most salient similarities and differences. Here are some sample prompts:

- Are spiders and insects more alike or more different?
- Are fractions and decimals more alike or more different?
- Are Ulysses S. Grant and Robert E. Lee more alike or more different?
- Are the heroines in these two stories more alike or more different?
- Are lithium and potassium more alike or more different?
- Are these two paintings more alike or more different?

Help students reflect on and analyze their decision-making process by calling attention to the criteria they use to make their choices. ("John argued that these paintings are more similar than different because their subject matter and color palette are almost identical. What criteria was Tameka using when she decided that the paintings were more different?")

Which Is More...Better...the Best...the Most?

This frame asks students to make and defend judgments based on quality or degree. Prompts contain comparative or superlative words such as *more*, *better*, *best*, *most*, and *greatest*. Here are some examples:

- Which is the best season: spring, summer, winter, or fall?
- Which of these articles provides the most realistic advice for dealing with bullying?
- Which type of graph is best for presenting this kind of data?
- Which is the most powerful line in this text?
- Which of these scientific discoveries had the greatest impact on world history?

Agree or Disagree?

With this frame, students are given debate-provoking statements rather than questions. Students decide whether they agree or disagree with each statement and then justify their decisions with appropriate evidence. Here are some sample statements:

- Children my age should have a set bedtime.
- The United States should adopt the metric system.
- This design plan is better than that one.
- Politicians are all the same; there's no real difference between Democrats and Republicans.

This or That?

This frame forces students to make a choice between two opposing characterizations of (or viewpoints on) a specific item, individual, or topic. Prompts take the form of questions like these:

- Is "playground time" useful time or a waste of time?
- Is Jay Gatsby a hero or a jerk?
- Is nuclear energy more helpful or harmful?
- Is teaching more of an art or a science?
- Do mobile devices in the classroom improve learning or interfere with learning?
- How should we remember the Age of Exploration—as a time of great discovery or a time of terrible exploitation?

As with all the frames in this tool, students are expected to support their positions with appropriate evidence.

Metaphorical Duels

Metaphorical Duels (Silver, Brunsting, Walsh, & Thomas, 2012) exploits the power of metaphorical thinking to promote depth of understanding. To use this frame, design two possible similes around a topic of interest, ask students which they feel is the most accurate, and have them justify their choices. Making the unusual connections that this frame requires forces students to think deeply and creatively about the critical attributes of the initial topic—a move that can have a powerful impact on comprehension and lead to truly insightful revelations.

Here are some sample prompts:

- Is a good friend more like a teddy bear or a flower?
- Is prejudice more like an iceberg or a runaway train?
- Is the circulatory system more like a bicycle or a delivery truck?
- Is the scientific method more like a recipe or a map?
- Are graphing calculators more like microscopes or telescopes?
- Are hieroglyphics more like a comic strip or a short story?

Encouraging students to describe the attributes of the items they're comparing can help them make more thoughtful and well-supported choices. ("Before deciding whether prejudice is more like an iceberg or a runaway train, jot down everything you know about prejudice, everything you know about icebergs, and everything you know about runaway trains.")

Physical Barometer

This frame, which is described more fully in the Interaction in an Instant tool (see p. 46), invites students to take a position on an issue, shore up their arguments with like-minded classmates, and then work to change the minds of classmates who hold different positions.

The Power of Pause

What is it?

A tool that highlights the power of simple pauses to promote thinking and learning

What are the benefits of using this tool?

Students live in a world that often values quick answers over quiet thought, "do it now" over deliberation, and "right this second" over reflection. Yet we know from the work of Art Costa and Bena Kallick (2008) that good thinkers are patient thinkers who know how to curtail their impulsivity and who practice metacognition by thinking about their thinking processes. Regular use of The Power of Pause develops these important habits of mind in students; it also helps teachers build a classroom culture in which thoughtful reflection (and the well-reasoned responses that result) is the norm. The tool teaches students to "hit the pause button" in a variety of learning contexts and for a variety of purposes, including reviewing and revising their work, monitoring and refocusing their attention, and assessing and addressing understanding gaps.

What are the basic steps?

1. Introduce the idea that when it comes to learning, faster isn't always better—that pausing to think can be extremely beneficial. Use questions like the ones below to help students begin to appreciate "the power of pause."

   - How might you benefit from pausing and thinking before responding to a question?
   - How might it help you to pause and think after reading each paragraph in a challenging text?
   - How might you benefit from pausing to reflect on your assignments before submitting them?

2. Explain that you'll be encouraging students to pause and think in a variety of different contexts over the course of the year—and that the goal in all cases is to help them achieve at higher levels.

3. Capitalize on the power of pause to improve academic achievement by building different types of pauses into your everyday classroom instruction. See pp. 100–102 for ideas.

4. Pause at the end of each "pausing lesson" to help students reflect on the power of pause. ("When did we pause? For what purpose? What did we do during the pause? How did it help us?")

5. Encourage students to "hit the pause button" without being told. ("Try pausing after every paragraph whenever you're reading a textbook, not just when I tell you to.")

   Tip: Prepare students to take this step by reviewing both *when* they might want to pause (e.g., after a question is posed, before submitting their work, at the end of a lecture) and *why* (e.g., to think through their ideas, review and revise their work, see what they do and don't understand).

6. Invite students to share and reflect on their experiences with using pauses independently. ("Describe when you've paused, what you've done or thought about during the pauses, and how pausing has made you a better learner.")

How is this tool used in the classroom?

✔ To help students recognize the power of pausing in different contexts

✔ To use pauses for the purpose of enhancing learning and achievement

✔ To develop key habits of mind, especially curtailing impulsivity and practicing metacognition

✔ To establish a classroom culture that invites and values thoughtful reflection

Teachers use this tool to help students appreciate—and benefit from—the power of pausing in different learning contexts. One student's thoughts about how pausing has helped her personally (the type of reflection called for in Step 6) are presented below.

When I pause I stop to think without rushing. I'm calm and take time to talk to myself.

Pausing helps me think of good ideas and answers. I can make better decisions!

When I pause I think about the task and what is clear and what is confusing.

Pausing helps me be a better thinker!

Pausing for Different Purposes[*]

Use the power of pause to help students recognize and signal you when they're lost

Prepare students to get more out of classroom lectures and lessons by PAUSING every five to ten minutes so they can REFLECT on how well they're following you. Students can let you know how they're doing using anything from simple hand signals (thumbs up or thumbs down) to "traffic light cards" (red, yellow, and green index cards used as described in the box below).

Hold up your red card to say, "Stop, I'm lost!"

Hold up your yellow card to say, "Slow down, I'm losing you!"

Hold up your green card to say, "Go forward, I've got this!"

Adjust instruction as needed based on the feedback that students provide. (Ask yourself, "Should I go back and reteach this material? Slow down? Keep doing what I'm doing?") Make a note of students who are struggling so you can work with them separately to bring them up to speed.

Use the power of pause to help students identify material that needs further study

Prepare students to become more self-directed learners by teaching them to identify and address areas of confusion. Train them to PAUSE at the end of lessons and reading assignments to THINK about what they did and didn't understand. Students can conduct these assessments in their heads, or they can communicate their findings using a "weather report" like the one below, which was inspired by Abigail Boutz et al.'s (2012) Clear or Cloudy? tool.

What do I understand CLEARLY?	What's still a bit CLOUDY?
Reptiles are cold-blooded. Reptiles ~~are~~ lay eggs. Reptiles have protective coverings like scales and turtle shells.	I'm still a little confused about what cold-blooded actually means.

Empower students to "clear up the cloudy areas" by discussing strategies they might try or resources that could help them. ("Today's lecture material is covered in Chapter 2 of your textbook. Read the chapter, and see me if you're still confused.") Or, work to clarify the confusion yourself using students' weather reports as a guide. Ask yourself who needs help with what, and then design your instruction accordingly. ("Hmmm ... Since a lot of students were confused about how to add mixed numbers, I should probably revisit that topic tomorrow" or "Since Tonya and Justin were the only ones having trouble, maybe I can work with them after class.")

---

[*]This section (pp. 100–102) presents seven different options for helping students capitalize on the power of pause. Within each option, the pauses—and the thinking/reflective behaviors that students should engage in during these pauses—are highlighted using ALL CAPS.

Use the power of pause to help students get more out of what they read

Help students improve their comprehension and retention of assigned reading materials by making them more active and reflective readers. Teach them to PAUSE after every paragraph, THINK about what they read, and SUMMARIZE the big ideas using a single sentence or sketch. Prepare students for success by modeling the stop-and-summarize process repeatedly and by discussing strategies they can use to distinguish important-to-summarize big ideas from smaller, less critical details.

Use the power of pause to encourage revision

Prepare students to produce higher-quality work by teaching them to PAUSE and REFLECT on their assignments before submitting them. Students can do a simple, self-directed skim (encourage them to fix what they find), or you can give them specific criteria for assessing and improving their work. In the case of a writing assignment, for example, you might ask students to read their pieces to themselves and check their work for The Seven Cs (adapted from Boutz et al., 2012):

Completeness: Did I leave out any words, details, or big ideas?

Coherence: Do my ideas make sense? Are they presented in a logical and orderly way?

Clarity: Are my ideas communicated clearly? Is my writing clear and easy to follow?

Correctness: Are there any spelling, grammar, punctuation, or factual errors that I can correct?

Composition: Are all the critical elements in place (e.g., claim, supporting details, conclusion)?

Congruence: Does my response address the assigned task or question?

Communication skills: Will my audience "get" what I wrote? Is my tone/language appropriate?

Prepare students for success by explaining assessment criteria in advance and providing models of exemplary work (e.g., an essay that fulfills the provided criteria).

Use the power of pause to invite thoughtful answers rather than impulsive ones

Help students develop high-quality responses to classroom questions by requiring them to PAUSE and THINK before answering. One way to do this is to reinforce a ten-second timeout between the time a question is posed and the time you ask for responses. Teach students to use the timeout as an opportunity to develop and refine their responses, either on their own or with a partner. Adjust the length of the pause as needed to fit the types of questions you pose.

Scaffold the process of developing a quality response by talking students through the timeout. Direct them to (1) check that they heard and understood the question, (2) put on their thinking caps, (3) jot down some possible ideas, and (4) refine their ideas with a partner. Creating icons for each of these four steps (see sample below) and pointing to the icons one by one can help students stay focused and productive during the pause.

Check that you heard and understood the question.	Put on your thinking cap.	Jot down possible ideas.	Discuss and refine your ideas with a partner.

Use the power of pause to help students identify and address lapses in attention

This technique (adapted from Harvey Silver et al.'s [2012] Attention Monitor tool) prepares students to acquire critical content by helping them pay better attention in class. To use it, PAUSE periodically while teaching and ask students to REFLECT on their level of focus. ("How well were you paying attention just now?") Have students indicate their level of attention using a simple show of fingers (e.g., thumbs up or thumbs down) or a rating scale ("attention monitor") like this one:

3 I am focused like a laser beam!	2 I am following along pretty well.	1 My attention is wandering a bit.	0 My attention is elsewhere.

Empower students to "C" their way back from lapses in attention by familiarizing them with these four simple strategies for refocusing:

Change your posture.	Clear your mind of distractions.	Create questions or notes.	Connect to the content.

Prepare students to implement these strategies successfully by explaining the strategies in student-friendly terms, modeling the strategies yourself, and posting visual reminders like the illustrated classroom poster above. Student-friendly explanations might sound something like this:

Change your posture: "Try sitting up straight, uncrossing your legs, and facing forward."

Clear your mind of distractions: "Think about what's distracting you—an argument with a friend, plans for the weekend, whatever. Tell yourself you're going to put this distraction out of your mind for now and wait until class is over to think about it again."

Create questions or notes: "Since it's easier to stay focused when you're actually doing something, force yourself to ask questions, answer questions, and/or take notes."

Connect to the content: "Make personal connections by asking, 'What do I know about this topic or text? Do I have any feelings or opinions about it? How is it relevant to me and my life?'"

Explain that the ultimate goal is for students to identify and address attention gaps on their own.

Use the power of pause to enhance students' problem-solving abilities

Help students become more strategic and successful problem solvers by training them to PAUSE and PLAN before they start working on a problem. Instruct students to read the problem carefully, reflect on what it's asking, and think through possible problem-solving strategies. Encourage students to PAUSE again when they're done working to REFLECT on the soundness of their solution, the effectiveness of their problem-solving strategy, and the accuracy of their work.

Clarify that this "pause and think before working" strategy can help students with all kinds of questions and prompts. Pausing to think through ideas and organizational strategies before responding to a writing prompt, for example, can help students develop higher-quality responses.

Power Previewing

What is it?

A tool that prepares students to better handle rigorous texts by teaching them to preview those texts in advance using a specially designed visual organizer

What are the benefits of using this tool?

We want all our students to become more powerful and self-sufficient readers. But what does that mean? Michael Pressley (2006), a leading researcher on reading instruction, tells us that "the conscious processing that is excellent reading begins before reading, continues during reading, and persists after reading is completed" (p. 57). Power Previewing is a tool that's designed to help every student develop the "conscious processing skills" of proficient readers, with special emphasis on before-reading skills, such as skimming for textual cues, making predictions, and determining how a text is structured. The tool teaches students what to do before they begin reading so that they are better able to understand, remember, and enjoy what they read.

What are the basic steps?

1. Distribute copies of the Power Previewing Organizer for nonfiction texts (p. 106).

Note: This tool was designed with nonfiction texts in mind, but you can use it with works of fiction as well. See Teacher Talk for details; see p. 107 for a fiction-specific organizer.

2. Use sample texts (e.g., articles, textbook passages) to explain and model the Power Previewing steps outlined below. Thoroughly review the "where to look for important information" section of the organizer so that students know where to look and what to pay attention to while skimming.

Prowl for clues: Look for important information as you skim through the text.

Pencil in key information: Record what you learn about the text's content and organization.

Pry open your memory: Ask yourself if anything in the text looks or sounds familiar.

Personalize the preview: Identify aspects of the text that you find interesting or challenging.

Predict what the text will be about: Use what you learn by skimming to make some predictions.

3. Have students use their organizers to preview a text that you or they select. Intervene as needed to help them make the most of the previewing process. Among other things, you can

- Ask guiding and focusing questions (e.g., "Do you see any recurring themes in this section?").
- Suggest strategies for addressing specific challenges (e.g., vocabulary strategies if challenging terms are the issue or strategies for figuring out what's important enough to write down).
- Encourage students to check their predictions when they read the text "for real."

4. Help students reflect on and learn from the previewing process. See Teacher Talk for ideas.

5. Remind students to use the Power Previewing strategy on their own, not just when you say so. To facilitate the process, post the Power Previewing steps in the classroom and give students copies of blank organizers to keep in their notebooks.

How is this tool used in the classroom?

✔ To teach students a strategy that they can use to get more out of rigorous texts

✔ To develop active and engaged readers who understand and enjoy what they read

EXAMPLE: The organizer below highlights the different kinds of things that a student might notice and comment on while previewing a nonfiction text (e.g., how the text is organized, recurring terms/ideas, themes with ties to previous units, items in illustrations and sidebars).

Where to look for important information:

- Titles, headings, and subheadings
- Opening paragraphs or introduction
- First and last sentence of each paragraph
- Summary paragraphs or lists of key points
- End-of-chapter or start-of-chapter questions
- Bold, italicized, and underlined information
- Circled, boxed, or highlighted information
- Graphs, figures, tables, charts, and maps
- Pictures, cartoons, and photographs
- Captions and figure legends

What are you previewing? What is it about (topic)?

A textbook chapter.
The title/topic is "Civilizations in the Americas."

How is the text structured or organized?

- The chapter is broken down into three major sections. Each one focuses on a different geographical region: Mesoamerica, South America, North America.
- Within these bigger sections, there are smaller subsections about each individual civilization.

What else did you notice or learn while skimming? What information and ideas seem to be important?

- The words "trade," "art," "geography," and "religion" appear in lots of different subsections.
- There are lots of pictures and sidebars about art, architecture, religion, and science.
- Several section headings and chapter questions focus on how geography impacted the civilizations.

Does anything look familiar or relate to something you've seen, read, learned about, or experienced?

- We talked about how geography impacts the development of civilizations in our unit on ancient Egypt.
- The art in some of the pictures looks like what we saw on our field trip to the museum.

What seems interesting?

- There are some interesting looking ceremonies.

What seems confusing or challenging? Do you know any strategies that can help you address these challenges?

- I might get the different civilizations mixed up. A graphic organizer might help me keep things organized.

What predictions can you make and why? (Check and mark the accuracy of your predictions as you read.)

- There's a lot on art and architecture, so I predict that these civilizations were known for those things.
- The word "trade" appears a lot, so I predict that trade was important to all these civilizations.

🌓 Teacher Talk

➔ Help students understand the rationale for using this tool by initiating a conversation about the benefits of skimming through (previewing) a text before actually reading it.

- Begin by having students describe the purpose of previews they are likely to be familiar with (e.g., movie previews, preseason sports previews, fashion previews in magazines).

- Ask students why it might be useful to preview texts before reading.

- Summarize and/or add to students' ideas. You might, for example, point out that knowing how a text is organized can make the information easier to understand and remember—or that generating predictions and personal connections can make reading more interactive and enjoyable.

➔ Don't assume the Power Previewing steps are self-explanatory. Explain and model each one thoroughly, making sure to "think aloud" as you work your way through sample texts. Continue modeling the previewing process until students are clear about how to find important information and complete their organizers on their own.

➔ In the beginning—or when using the tool with younger students, struggling readers, or English language learners—preview texts as a class and use guiding questions to focus students' attention on what's important. For example, "Does anything on this page look like something we've seen before?" or "Do you notice any words that look different than the others? Why might the author have done that?" Once you've flipped through the entire text, review the questions on the organizer as a class. Have students speak their answers aloud or write (or draw) them on the organizer.

➔ Having students highlight the important information that they find while prowling and/or turn in their organizers at the end of the lesson can help you identify individuals who need extra help.

➔ Help students reflect on and learn from the previewing process (Step 4) using questions like these: How did you prowl? What did you learn by previewing? How did previewing affect what you paid attention to while reading? Did previewing make the text more enjoyable or easier to understand? Might it be useful to preview texts on your own? Why or why not?

➔ Previewing the structure and organization of a text can be as helpful as previewing the content. For this reason, it's a good idea to familiarize students with common text structures (e.g., problem-solution, comparison, cause-effect, claim/evidence, chronological sequence) and encourage them to prowl for those structures as they skim. Reviewing "tip-off words" that signal different kinds of texts (e.g., *first*, *second*, and *finally* for a chronologically or sequentially structured text) can help.

➔ If you want students to preview works of fiction instead of nonfiction texts, give them fiction-specific organizers. Use the organizer on p. 107 as is, or modify it as needed to fit your selected text type (e.g., illustrated versus not illustrated, chapter book versus no chapters). Offer students guidance about what to focus on while skimming fiction (e.g., elements like illustrations and chapter titles rather than of end-of-chapter questions and summary paragraphs). You might ask younger students to do a "picture walk" (look at a book's illustrations, describe what they notice, and make predictions based on what they see). You might have older students skim a few paragraphs to get a sense of an author's writing style or use chapter titles to make predictions about overall plot or theme.

Power Previewing Organizer (nonfiction)

Where to look for important information:
- Titles, headings, and subheadings
- Opening paragraphs or introduction
- First and last sentence of each paragraph
- Summary paragraphs or lists of key points
- End-of-chapter or start-of-chapter questions
- Bold, italicized, and underlined information
- Circled, boxed, or highlighted information
- Graphs, figures, tables, charts, and maps
- Pictures, cartoons, and photographs
- Captions and figure legends

What are you previewing? What is it about (topic)?

How is the text structured or organized?

What else did you notice or learn while skimming? What information and ideas seem to be important?

Does anything look familiar or relate to something you've seen, read, learned about, or experienced?

What seems interesting?

What seems confusing or challenging? Do you know any strategies that can help you address these challenges?

What predictions can you make and why? (Check and mark the accuracy of your predictions as you read.)

Power Previewing Organizer (fiction)

What to look at as you skim:
- Title and author
- Front and back cover
- Pictures
- Opening lines or paragraphs
- Chapter titles
- Text that looks "different" (for example, a different size or style)
- Anything else that stands out

What are you previewing? What is its title?

Who is the author?

What did you see or notice while skimming?

Did anything look familiar or interesting?

What do you think this reading will be about? What do you think might happen?

Check your ideas after you finish reading.

Epilogue: Looking Back to Go Forward

At this point in the book, we've done what we set out to do. We've outlined the Four Cornerstones of an Effective Classroom and provided tools you can use to lay these cornerstones in place. Now it's up to you to try the tools in your classroom, reflect on how well they work, and think about steps you can take to get them working even better.

The reflection form on the next page was designed to help you look back on your practice and use what you learn to establish concrete plans for improvement. We encourage you to use the form regularly and save your responses, along with copies of relevant artifacts (e.g., lesson plans, handouts, classroom posters, samples of student work). Creating this kind of "reflection journal" will enable you to look back on and learn from your experiences, document growth over time (yours and your students'), and share what you've been doing with colleagues and/or supervisors. A sample journal entry is shown below.

REFLECTING ON MY PRACTICE

1) What tool did I use? On what date? With what group of students or class?

   I used the Power Previewing tool with the entire class on October 12th.

2) Have I used this tool before? No.

3) How did I build the tool into my lesson plans? And for what purpose?

   I used the organizer to have students preview an article about why honeybees are disappearing. My goal was to help them really engage with the text and get more out of it than they usually do when I assign these kinds of articles.

4) Did I use the tool as written or modify it in any way? (Explain any modifications.) Used as is.

5) What worked well? What (if any) issues or challenges did I face?

   Students were definitely examining the text more closely than usual, but many of them seemed overwhelmed by the text and the organizer. In particular, they didn't seem confident about where to look for important information or what to write down.

6) What might I do differently the next time I use this tool to make it work even better?

   I should've used a shorter and simpler article the first time. I will make sure to do that next time. I will also spend some additional time reviewing the text features that are described in the "P" of the organizer so students are clearer about where to look for important information. And I will do some more modeling and practicing as a class.

7) How did the tool affect me, my students, and/or our classroom environment?

   (Did it affect factors like engagement, effort, or collaboration? Did it promote better behavior, thinking, or learning? Did it enhance my teaching, my relationships with students, or the classroom environment?)

   My better readers were really focused and deeply interacting with the text while working on their organizers. Even the students who were struggling were examining the text more closely than I expected.

8) Would I use this tool again and/or recommend it to a colleague? Why or why not?

   Yes, because I think it has real potential to promote more focused and active reading — and a better understanding of assigned texts. It's also a good tool for reviewing critical text features. I think the issues I encountered resulted from picking an overly difficult text and not doing enough reviewing and modeling. I thought our previous lessons on text features would've carried over, but I should've reviewed to be sure.

Reflecting On My Practice

1) What tool did I use? On what date? With what group of students or class?

2) Have I used this tool before?

3) How did I build the tool into my lesson plans? And for what purpose?

4) Did I use the tool as written or modify it in any way? (Explain any modifications.)

5) What worked well? What (if any) issues or challenges did I face?

6) What might I do differently the next time I use this tool to make it work even better?

7) How did the tool affect me, my students, and/or our classroom environment?

   (Did it affect factors like engagement, effort, or collaboration? Did it promote better behavior, thinking, or learning? Did it enhance my teaching, my relationships with students, or the classroom environment?)

8) Would I use this tool again and/or recommend it to a colleague? Why or why not?

Appendix: An Overview of the Thoughtful Classroom Teacher Effectiveness Framework

The Thoughtful Classroom Teacher Effectiveness Framework (Silver Strong & Associates, 2012) is a comprehensive system for observing, evaluating, and refining classroom practice. It synthesizes a wide body of research on instructional design and teacher effectiveness, as well as insight from hundreds of teachers and administrators across the United States. The ultimate goal of the framework is to create a common language for talking about high-quality teaching and how classroom practice can be improved.

The framework contains three distinct domains: (1) The Four Cornerstones of Effective Classrooms, which are the focus of this book; (2) The Five Episodes of Effective Instruction; and (3) Effective Professional Practice.* Each domain is briefly explained in the figure below.

DOMAIN ONE
Four Cornerstones of Effective Classrooms
(Dimensions 1, 2, 3, & 4)

Around the framework are four foundational dimensions that have been adapted from preeminent teacher-effectiveness models (Danielson, 2007; Marzano, 2007; Marzano, Frontier, & Livingston, 2011; Saphier, Haley-Speca, & Gower, 2008; Stronge, 2010). These are the four dimensions:

1 Organization, Rules, and Procedures

2 Positive Relationships

3 Engagement and Enjoyment

4 A Culture of Thinking and Learning

These dimensions, or cornerstones, represent the universal elements of quality instruction, whether in a kindergarten class, AP Physics lab, or anywhere in between. Without these cornerstones in place, student learning will be compromised.

DOMAIN TWO
Five Episodes of Effective Instruction
(Dimensions 5, 6, 7, 8, & 9)

While there are clear universal elements to good instruction, it is also true that good instruction tends to unfold in a series of distinct learning episodes. By synthesizing the best research on instructional design (Hunter, 1984; Marzano, 2007; Wiggins & McTighe, 2005), we've identified five critical episodes that increase the likelihood of deep learning. In these five episodes, teachers work toward distinct instructional purposes:

5 Preparing Students for New Learning

6 Presenting New Learning

7 Deepening and Reinforcing Learning

8 Applying Learning

9 Reflecting On and Celebrating Learning

Understanding these five episodes—and their driving purposes—is critical for both the teacher and the observer. Teachers use these episodes to design high-quality lessons and units. For classroom observations, these five episodes immediately orient the observer within the instructional sequence, ensuring that teachers and observers are on the same page.

The Thoughtful Classroom Teacher Effectiveness Framework

Organization, Rules, and Procedures	Preparing Students for New Learning	Positive Relationships
Deepening and Reinforcing Learning	Presenting New Learning	Reflecting On and Celebrating Learning
A Culture of Thinking and Learning	Applying Learning	Engagement and Enjoyment

Professional Practice

DOMAIN THREE
Effective Professional Practice: Looking Beyond the Classroom (Dimension 10)

10 The framework also includes a tenth dimension focused on professional practice, which addresses important non-instructional responsibilities, including the teacher's commitment to ongoing learning, professionalism, and the school community.

*Tools for addressing the first domain of the Thoughtful Classroom Teacher Effectiveness Framework ("The Four Cornerstones") can be found in this book, *Tools for a Successful School Year*. Tools that support the second domain of the framework ("The Five Episodes of Effective Instruction") are available in *Tools for Thoughtful Assessment* (Boutz et al., 2012).

References

Akey, T. M. (2006). *School context, student attitudes and behavior, and academic achievement: An exploratory analysis.* New York: MDRC. Retrieved from http://www.mdrc.org/publication/student-context-student-attitudes-and-behavior-and-academic-achievement

Alderman, M. K. (2008). *Motivation for achievement: Possibilities for teaching and learning* (3rd ed.). New York: Routledge.

Aronson, E., Blaney, N., Stephin, C., Sikes, J., & Snapp, M. (1978). *The jigsaw classroom.* Beverly Hills, CA: Sage.

Boutz, A. L., Silver, H. F., Jackson, J. W., & Perini, M. J. (2012). *Tools for thoughtful assessment: Classroom-ready techniques for improving teaching and learning.* Franklin Lakes, NJ: Thoughtful Education Press.

Boynton, S. (2011). *Happy hippo, angry duck: A book of moods.* New York: Little Simon.

Carnegie, D. (1998). *How to win friends and influence people.* New York: Gallery Books. (Original work published 1936)

Confucius. (n.d.). *Confucius quotes.* Retrieved from http://www.brainyquote.com/quotes/quotes/c/confucius136804.html

Costa, A. L., & Kallick, B. (Eds.). (2008). *Learning and leading with habits of mind: 16 essential characteristics for success.* Alexandria, VA: ASCD.

Council of Chief State School Officers. (2011). *Interstate Teacher Assessment and Support Consortium (InTASC) Model Core Teaching Standards: A Resource for State Dialogue.* Washington, DC: Author.

Danielson, C. (2007). *Enhancing professional practice: A framework for teaching* (2nd ed.). Alexandria, VA: ASCD.

Danielson, C. (2013). *The framework for teaching evaluation instrument.* Princeton, NJ: The Danielson Group.

Dweck, C. S. (1975). The role of expectations and attributions in the alleviation of learned helplessness. *Journal of Personality and Social Psychology, 31*(4), 674–685.

Dweck, C. S. (2007a). *Mindset: The new psychology of success.* New York: Random House.

Dweck, C. S. (2007b). The perils and promises of praise. *Educational Leadership, 65*(2), 34–39.

Fogarty, R. (2008). Foreword. In A. L. Costa, *The school as a home for the mind: Creating mindful curriculum, instruction, and dialogue* (2nd ed., pp. vi–vii). Thousand Oaks, CA: Corwin Press.

Gandhi, I. (n.d.). *Indira Gandhi quotes.* Retrieved from http://www.brainyquote.com/quotes/quotes/i/indiragand100042.html

Gordon, T. (1974). *Teacher effectiveness training.* New York: Wyden.

Guilford, J. P. (1950). Creativity. *American Psychologist, 5*(9), 444–454.

Hanson, R. J., Dewing, R. T., Silver, H. F., & Strong, R. W. (1991, March). *In our reach: Identifying and working more effectively with at-risk learners.* Paper presented at the ASCD Annual Conference, San Francisco, CA.

Haystead, M. W., & Marzano, M. J. (2009). *Meta-analytic synthesis of studies conducted at Marzano Research Laboratory on instructional strategies.* Englewood, CO: Marzano Research Laboratory.

Holmes, B. (2014, May 12). Hone the top 5 soft skills every college student needs [Blog post]. Retrieved from www.usnews.com/education/blogs/college-admissions-playbook/2014/05/12/hone-the-top-5-soft-skills-every-college-student-needs

Hunter, M. (1984). Knowing, teaching, and supervising. In P. Hosford (Ed.), *Using what we know about teaching* (pp. 169–192). Alexandria, VA: ASCD.

Johnson, R., & Johnson, D. W. (1994). An overview of cooperative learning. In J. Thousand, R. Villa, & A. Nevin (Eds.). *Creativity and collaborative learning* (pp. 31–44). Baltimore: Brooks.

Keller, H. (n.d.). *Helen Keller quotes*. Retrieved from http://www.brainyquote.com/quotes/quotes/h /helenkelle382259.html

Keller, L. (2007). *Do unto otters: A book about manners*. New York: Holt.

Lowry, N., & Johnson, D. W. (1981). Effects of controversy on epistemic curiosity, achievement, and attitudes. *The Journal of Social Psychology, 115*(1), 31–43.

Lyman, F. (1981). The responsive classroom discussion: The inclusion of all students. In A. Anderson (Ed.), *Mainstreaming digest* (pp. 109–113). College Park: University of Maryland.

Marzano, R. J. (2007). *The art and science of teaching: A comprehensive framework for effective instruction*. Alexandria, VA: ASCD.

Marzano, R. J. (2010). Using games to enhance student achievement. *Educational Leadership, 67*(5), 71–72.

Marzano, R. J. (2013). *The Marzano teacher evaluation model*. Bloomington, IN: Marzano Research Laboratory.

Marzano, R. J., Frontier, T., & Livingston, D. (2011). *Effective supervision: Supporting the art and science of teaching*. Alexandria, VA: ASCD.

Milne, A. A. (n.d.). *A. A. Milne quotes*. Retrieved from http://www.brainyquote.com/quotes/quotes/a/aamilne121656 .html

Moss, C. M., & Brookhart, S. M. (2009). *Advancing formative assessment in every classroom: A guide for instructional leaders*. Alexandria, VA: ASCD.

National Governors Association Center for Best Practices, Council of Chief State School Officers. (2010a). *Common Core State Standards for English language arts & literacy in history/social studies, science, and technical subjects*. Washington, DC: Author.

National Governors Association Center for Best Practices, Council of Chief State School Officers. (2010b). *Common Core State Standards for mathematics*. Washington, DC: Author.

Nelson, J. (1985). The three R's of logical consequences, the three R's of punishment, and the six steps for winning children over. *Individual Psychology, 41*(2), 161–165.

NGSS Lead States (2013). *Next Generation Science Standards: For states, by states*. Washington, DC: The National Academies Press.

Pashler, H., Bain, P., Bottge, B., Graesser, A., Koedinger, K., McDaniel, M., & Metcalfe, J. (2007). *Organizing instruction and study to improve student learning: IES practice guide* (NCER 2007–2004). Washington, DC: National Center for Education Research, Institute of Education Sciences, US Department of Education. Retrieved from ERIC (ED498555).

Pressley, M. (2006). *Reading instruction that works: The case for balanced teaching* (3rd ed.). New York: The Guilford Press.

Raphael, L. M., Pressley, M., & Mohan, L. (2008). Engaging instruction in middle school classrooms: An observational study of nine teachers. *Elementary School Journal, 109* (1), 61–81.

Saphier, J., Haley-Speca, M. A., & Gower, R. (2008). *The skillful teacher: Building your teaching skills* (6th ed.). Acton, MA: Research for Better Teaching.

Sears, N. (n.d.). *Building relationships with students*. Retrieved from http://www.nea.org/tools/29469.htm

Silver, H. F., & Boutz, A. L. (2015). *Tools for conquering the Common Core: Classroom-ready techniques for targeting the ELA/literacy standards*. Franklin Lakes, NJ: Thoughtful Education Press.

Silver, H. F., Brunsting, J. R., Walsh, T., & Thomas, E. J. (2012). *Math tools, grades 3–12: 60+ ways to build mathematical practices, differentiate instruction, and increase student engagement* (2nd ed.). Thousand Oaks, CA: Corwin Press.

Silver, H. F., Hanson, J. R., Strong, R. W., & Schwartz, P. B. (1996). *Teaching styles and strategies* (3rd ed.). Trenton, NJ: Thoughtful Education Press.

Silver, H. F., & Perini, M. J. (2010a). *Classroom curriculum design: How strategic units improve instruction and engage students in meaningful learning.* Ho-Ho-Kus, NJ: Thoughtful Education Press.

Silver, H. F., & Perini, M. J. (2010b). The eight Cs of engagement: How learning styles and instructional design increase student commitment to learning. In R. J. Marzano (Ed.), *On excellence in teaching* (pp. 319–344). Bloomington, IN: Solution Tree Press.

Silver, H. F., Strong, R. W., and Perini, M. J. (2007) *The strategic teacher: Selecting the right research-based strategy for every lesson.* Alexandria, VA: ASCD.

Silver Strong & Associates. (2012). *The thoughtful classroom teacher effectiveness framework: Resource guide.* Franklin Lakes, NJ: Author.

Simonsen, B., Fairbanks, S., Briesch, A., Myers, D., & Sugai, G. (2008). Evidence-based practices in classroom management: Considerations for research to practice. *Education and Treatment of Children, 31*(2), 351–380.

Simonsen, B., & Myers, D. (2015). *Classwide positive behavior interventions and supports: A guide to proactive classroom management.* New York: The Guilford Press.

Stronge, J. H. (2010). *Evaluating what good teachers do: Eight research-based standards for assessing teacher excellence.* Larchmont, NY: Eye on Education.

Tomlinson, C. A., & Imbeau, M. B. (2010). *Leading and managing a differentiated classroom.* Alexandria, VA: ASCD.

US Office of Special Education Programs. (2015). *Supporting and responding to behavior: Evidence-based classroom strategies for teachers.* Retrieved from http://www.pbis.org/common/cms/files/pbisresources/Supporting%20and%20Responding%20to%20Behavior.pdf

Wiggins, G. P., & McTighe, J. (2005). *Understanding by design* (2nd ed.). Alexandria, VA: ASCD.

Wong, H. K., & Wong, R. T. (with Jondahl, S. F., & Ferguson, O. F.). (2014). *The classroom management book.* Mountain View, CA: Harry K. Wong Publications, Inc.

Index of Tools

About the Authors

Harvey F. Silver, EdD, cofounder and president of Silver Strong & Associates, has more than forty years of experience as a teacher, administrator, and consultant. He is a regular speaker at national and regional educational conferences, addressing a wide range of topics, including differentiated instruction, thoughtful assessment, school leadership, strategies for conquering the Common Core, and lesson/unit design. Dr. Silver also conducts workshops for schools, districts, and educational organizations throughout North America. He is the co-author of several educational bestsellers, including *Tools for Thoughtful Assessment*; *Tools for Promoting Active, In-Depth Learning*; and *The Core Six*, a book of research-based strategies for addressing the Common Core State Standards. He also has collaborated with Matthew J. Perini to develop the Thoughtful Classroom Teacher Effectiveness Framework, a comprehensive teacher evaluation system that is being implemented in school districts across the country.

Matthew J. Perini, senior director of content development for Silver Strong & Associates, has authored numerous books, curriculum guides, and articles on a wide range of topics, including reading instruction, formative assessment, and effective teaching practices. Most recently, he has collaborated with Harvey Silver, R. Thomas Dewing, and ASCD on *The Core Six*, a book of research-based strategies for addressing the Common Core State Standards. He also has been a driving force in the development of ASCD and Silver Strong & Associates' Strategic Teacher Initiative and the Thoughtful Classroom Teacher Effectiveness Framework.

Abigail L. Boutz, PhD, has taught, tutored, and mentored students at the elementary through college levels, most recently at the University of California, Los Angeles, where she served as a lecturer for the Life Sciences Department, a university field supervisor for the Teacher Education Program, and an academic coordinator for the Undergraduate Research Center / Center for Academic and Research Excellence. During her tenure with Silver Strong & Associates, she has designed training modules and workshop materials on classroom tools and strategies, learning styles, and instructional leadership. She also has co-authored two award-winning titles in the Tools for Today's Educators series: *Tools for Thoughtful Assessment* and *Tools for Conquering the Common Core*.

Notes